The
Color
Complex

*The Politics of Skin Color
Among African Americans*

The Color Complex

The Politics of Skin Color
Among African Americans

Kathy Russell
Midge Wilson, Ph.D.
Ronald Hall, Ph.D.

ANCHOR BOOKS
DOUBLEDAY
New York London Toronto Sydney Auckland

AN ANCHOR BOOK

PUBLISHED BY DOUBLEDAY

a division of Bantam Doubleday Dell Publishing Group, Inc.
1540 Broadway, New York, New York 10036

ANCHOR BOOKS, DOUBLEDAY, and the portrayal of an anchor
are trademarks of Doubleday, a division of Bantam Doubleday Dell
Publishing Group, Inc.

*The names of some of the people who appear in this book, along with details of their
lives, have been changed to protect their privacy. Each such instance is noted in the
text the first time the person appears.*

The Color Complex was originally published in hardcover by Harcourt Brace
Jovanovich in 1992. The Anchor Books edition is published by arrangement with
Harcourt Brace Jovanovich.

Library of Congress Cataloging-in-Publication Data

Russell, Kathy.
The color complex: the politics of skin color among African
Americans/Kathy Russell, Midge Wilson, Ronald Hall.—1st Anchor Books ed.
    p. cm.
Includes bibliographical references (p.) and index.
1. Afro-Americans—Race identity. 2. Black race—Color—Social
aspects—United States. I. Wilson, Midge. II. Hall, Ronald E.
III. Title.
[E185.625.R79 1993]
305.896'073—dc20 93-13294
CIP

ISBN 0-385-47161-0
Copyright © 1992 by Kathy Y. Russell, Midge Wilson, and Ronald E. Hall
All Rights Reserved
Printed in the United States of America
First Anchor Books Edition: November 1993

10 9 8 7 6 5

This book is dedicated
to Kathy's mother, Dorothy C. Russell,
and Midge's husband, Shaun D. Reynolds,
for their unwavering love and support.

Contents

Introduction

Intraracial color discrimination is an embarrassing and controversial subject for African Americans. While many prefer not to discuss it, especially in the company of Whites, others contend that skin color bias no longer exists—that it's history, water over the dam. Yet beneath a surface appearance of Black solidarity lies a matrix of attitudes about skin color and features in which color, not character, establishes friendships, degree of lightness, not expertise, influences hiring; and complexion, not talent, dictates casting for television and film. In the world of entertainment, a Black superstar has surgically altered his features to the point where he no longer looks Black. Delve a little deeper, and you will find a reservoir of guilt and anger that threatens to overflow, exposing to African Americans the truth— that skin color still matters.

During the 1980s Black filmmaker Spike Lee directed, produced, and starred in a musical, *School Daze,* about obsession with skin color on a Black college campus. Although he was criticized by some members of his own community for "airing their dirty laundry," Lee returned to the subject in *Jungle Fever,* which also explored the passions of interracial sexual liaisons. In *Jungle Fever,* a dark-skinned Black man named Flipper (Wesley Snipes) is happily married to a lighter-skinned Black woman, Drew (Lonette McKee), until he becomes sexually involved with his White secretary, Angie (Annabella Sciorra). When Drew discovers the affair her temper flares, not so much because her husband has been unfaithful but because he

1

has been unfaithful with a White woman. In a pivotal scene, she rails:

> . . . What I mean is you've got a complex about color. You've always had it. I never wanted to believe it until now. . . . I told you what happened to me when I was growing up . . . I told you how they called me high yella, yellow bitch. White honky, honky white, white nigger, nigger white, octoroon, quadroon, half-breed, mongrel . . .

In telling Flipper he has a complex about color, Drew is accusing him of an old prejudice among Blacks, a prejudice she knows intimately because she looks White.

Traditionally, the color complex involved light-skinned Blacks' rejection of Blacks who were darker. Increasingly, however, the color complex shows up in the form of dark-skinned African Americans spurning their lighter-skinned brothers and sisters for not being Black enough. The complex even includes attitudes about hair texture, nose shape, and eye color. In short, the "color complex" is a psychological fixation about color and features that leads Blacks to discriminate against each other. Because the color complex has long been considered unmentionable, it has been called the "last taboo" among African Americans.

The color complex may reveal itself in a variety of ways wherever Blacks come together—in families, at work, in social situations. An uncensored comment may slip unexpectedly into a conversation, wreaking emotional havoc. An insensitive relative may criticize a Black child for having a "nappy head." A Black supervisor may create tension in the office by harping on a subordinate's lighter skin color, saying he or she has had it "too easy." The revelation of a hidden bias may even bring a promising relationship to an end, as when one attractive medium-toned Black woman in her twenties discovered that the man she had fallen in love with had a problem with her color.

> It was our third date, and following a romantic dinner, over dessert, I caught what I thought was Carl's approving gaze.

Demurely, I inquired, "What's making you smile so?" "You know," he paused and then continued, "you're pretty smart and you're a lotta fun but . . . I just can't get too serious with a dark-skinned woman. It's important to me to have light-skinned children." I watched as he then casually stuffed in his mouth the last piece of vanilla cream pie laden with chocolate sauce. My own dinner churned inside while the blood rushed to my face. I felt like the blackest, ugliest sister alive, and hated him for making me feel that way. With all the dignity I could muster, I got up, and walked across that restaurant and out the door.

Whites who are unaware of the color complex may be puzzled when they first encounter it. One White therapist recalls her initial confusion when a young Black female client began describing her painful home life, all the while nervously twisting and knotting her long, thick black hair.

"My sisters hate me," she cried. "But it is not my fault. When company comes over, my Papa, who's so proud of this long, straight hair of mine, makes me come sit in the dining room with him and his friends. My sisters, who have kinda short 'n' nappy hair, have to stay in the kitchen." "I'm sorry, I don't understand," the therapist said. She further explained, "He likes to show me off, like I'm some sorta trophy or something. The thing is, I hate my hair." She sobbed, "I'd rather my sisters liked me."

Most Blacks are careful about letting Whites in on their "dirty little secret." But Whites ought not to be isolated from the concerns of Blacks, especially since they so often have the power to hire, promote, appoint, and elect them. In a multicultural society like our own, justifications for hiding the color complex no longer hold weight. Blacks and Whites regularly attend school together, work in the same offices, and share the same neighborhoods. Ignorance of another's culture only breeds racism.

It is wise to remember that prejudice of any kind creates systems of privilege as well as oppression. Skin-color bias is no different; while many Blacks are hurt by colorism, others benefit from it. In today's climate of political correctness, it is downright fashionable to be able to claim the status of a victim. Yet often the individual members of an oppressed group conveniently ignore the benefits they may receive from simultaneous membership in another group. For example, if a White female incessantly complains about sexism without acknowledging the privilege that comes from being White, she misses the larger issue. Similarly, if light-skinned, keen-featured Blacks talk only of prejudice from Whites, without examining how their own color and features grant them social and economic advantages, both within and outside their own community, they, too, risk perpetuating a social hierarchy based on appearance.

The Color Complex grew out of the personal experiences and observations of its three authors. Kathy Russell, a Black woman with fairly light skin and long hair, often detected skin and feature discrimination as an adolescent but was unable to put a finger on exactly what it was she was experiencing. She knew only that her features had the power to make others see her either as popular and attractive, with "some pretty, long hair," or as a snob and a social outcast, rejected for acting too "white-like." In high school, some of the darker-skinned students even taunted her: "You think you bad cuz you got some hair."

Later, as an adult, Kathy began to think seriously about the social significance of these experiences, including the color-conscious comments she so often heard: "She's kinda cute for a dark-skinned girl" or "Don't bring home any old dark-skinned Black boys, cause I don't want any Black, nappy-headed grandbabies." While aware that these attitudes existed, she failed to comprehend why her own people felt so strongly about skin color.

When Kathy attempted to research color bias, she soon bumped up against old attitudes. "I wouldn't mess with that," she was told. "Just one more thing for White people to use against us." Instead of discouraging her, such comments only motivated her to learn more about the issue. She also began a one-person crusade to confront skin-color prejudice whenever she encountered it, challenging statements about the superiority of light skin or claims to an African heritage based on color alone. And she longed to help repair the damage done to all her Black sisters who had been made to feel ugly and ashamed for having dark skin and kinky hair.

Kathy looked for books on the subject and found none. Pondering the idea of filling the information gap by writing her own book on the color complex, she searched for coauthors who could complement and augment her views. This search led her first to Midge Wilson, a professor of women's studies and psychology at DePaul University, and then to Ronald Hall, who teaches social work at Augsburg College in Minneapolis.

Midge Wilson, a feminist social psychologist, had established her career by conducting research on attitudes about discriminatory physical attractiveness, primarily as they affect White women. Then, in the mid-1980s, a Black graduate student asked her to serve as adviser for a dissertation on the stereotyping of African-American women on the basis of their skin color and features. Suddenly Midge was exposed to a whole new cultural phenomenon, and she, too, began to investigate culturally relevant aspects of appearance in Blacks. She realized that many other Whites were probably unaware of the extent of skin-color bias within the Black community and, like herself, would benefit from becoming better educated about it. Not that Whites do not have their own color stereotypes about Blacks: having grown up in the South, Midge recalls hearing all the myths, including the "mulatto hypothesis"—the theory that light-skinned Blacks were intellectually superior because of their White blood—and being aware that dark-skinned Negro men were consciously or unconsciously considered more criminally dangerous and sexually driven than those lighter-skinned.

Midge and her former student went on to publish an article about the psychology of skin color that addressed clinical issues of the color complex for Black women. Later, Midge was asked to serve as an expert witness in a court case on intraracial color discrimination in

Atlanta in January 1990. There she met Ronald Hall, who, because of his extensive research on the subject, was also asked to serve as a expert witness in the same case.

Ronald Hall grew up in Philadelphia, in a family of widely varying skin colors, but he was not particularly aware of color bias within the Black community. Although he was certainly attuned to differences between Blacks, he had always assumed that they were based more on class than on color. Later, when he went south to attend graduate school in social work, Ron was struck by the fact that even across different socioeconomic classes students of the same skin color gravitated toward each other. He had originally planned to do his doctoral research on racism, but his observations led him to investigate the topic of skin color instead.

Ron's reading and empirical research led him to the conclusion that color prejudice was a potent force in the Black community. By the time he and Midge met in Atlanta, he had begun work on a manuscript entitled *The Bleaching Syndrome,* about the clinical implications of skin color for those Blacks who desire lighter skin.

We believe that there are significant advantages to bringing together the three perspectives of a Black woman, a White woman, and a Black man on the enormously sensitive topic of skin color and feature discrimination among Blacks. Each of us has noticed things that the others might have missed. Working as a threesome has, of course, presented some stylistic challenges. Among other things, we had long debates over what to call the population about which we were writing. During the past several years the use of African American has become more politically acceptable than Black, especially in such formal contexts as books, articles, lectures, and news reports. Yet Black remains popular because of its linguistic simplicity. We are also aware that some in the Black community reject the phrase African American, so we have compromised. As the reader will notice, we use African American and Black interchangeably, and, where historically appropriate, we occasionally employ Negro and Colored.

Another word that gave us trouble, and one for which we found no adequate substitute, was "mulatto." The word, denoting a person of mixed Black and White heritage, is Spanish in origin and means nothing more than "hybrid," but because of its association with slavery it has a derogatory implication. The word "mule" is similarly derived from the Spanish for "hybrid," and came to serve as a metaphor for a cross between the refined White plantation owner (thoroughbred horse) and the lowly, inferior Black slave (donkey). Where historically appropriate, we have retained "mulatto," but in contemporary references we use such phrases as "multicultural" or "of mixed heritage."

This book attempts to raise awareness among both Blacks *and* Whites about the color complex. We offer it as a step toward ending color prejudice. In writing it we have synthesized history, social science research, Black literature, and interviews with Black scholars, novelists, actors, film directors, business leaders, and persons in the media.

The Color Complex is not meant to be prescriptive. It does not denounce interracial marriage or berate Blacks for using hair-straightening products or wearing colored contact lenses. People's appearances and love lives are their own business, and should remain so. Yet we share the conviction that an informed individual can make choices more freely and can better resist social practices and cultural attitudes that are meaningless and unfair.

1. Masters, Slaves, and Lovers

Next comes a warmer race, from sable sprung,
To love each thought, to lust each nerve is strung;
The Samboe dark, and the Mulatto brown,
The Mestize fair, the well-limb'd Quadroon,
And jetty Afric, from no spurious sire,
Warm as her soil, and as her sun—on fire.
These sooty dames, well vers'd in Venus' school,
Make love an art, and boast they kiss by rule.
—"Jamaica, a Poem in Three Parts," London, 1777;
    published in the *South Carolina Gazette*

To trace the origins of the color complex, we must return to the year 1607 when three ships sailed into Chesapeake Bay, stopping at Jamestown, Virginia, to establish the first English colony in the New World. As natives watched, pale-skinned strangers cleared the wilderness, built forts, and planted crops. More White men followed, but to survive, the tiny settlement needed women and a reliable supply of cheap labor. A full twelve years passed before the first White women disembarked at Jamestown, and in that same year the first shipment of Africans arrived, too.

It was a new land and a new era filled with possibilities. What might have been unthinkable in Europe and Africa was an everyday occurrence in the wilderness. Miscegenation, or race mixing, became widespread as Europeans, Africans, and Native Americans mixed their seed and substance to produce a kaleidoscope of skin tones and features. But these primary race groupings differed sharply in their civil liberties and political freedoms. Subtle variations in appearance took on enormous consequence in meaning, especially among Negroes. Against a backdrop of love and rape, politics and war, and, ultimately, power and privilege, attitudes about skin color evolved in America.

After the long and treacherous transatlantic voyage to an uncertain and often dangerous destination, English sailors arrived in the New World desperate for rest and recreation. Native women were seduced or raped, and before long the first generation of blue-eyed, light-skinned Indians appeared among the local tribes. Little is known about these early mixed-breed natives, since their numbers were quite small. With the exception of a few isolated fur trappers on the frontier, English settlers and Indians rarely seemed to trust each other long enough to mate.

The Indians were particularly resentful of the White man's attempts to enslave them. For the most part, they managed to resist. The natives knew the land far better than the Europeans did, and if captured they could easily escape and hide. It became apparent that the English would have to find some other source of cheap labor if their settlement was to become permanent.

Dutch traders provided the answer. They brought Africans to Virginia from Santo Domingo in the West Indies, where Negroes had been enslaved on sugar plantations since the 1500s. Among this first group of Africans to set foot in America were a few who were English speaking and some who had even been converted to Christianity. The early White Virginians, unfamiliar with the nuances of slavery, released religious converts following a specified term of service. From the earliest years of the colonies, then, there were Negroes who lived free.

Any Christian concern about the morality of slavery receded as the idea of having a permanent labor force gained popular acceptance. Laws were hurriedly passed to ensure the rights of colonists who wished to keep their servants for life. In 1667, Virginia declared that a person could be both Christian and enslaved, thereby discouraging slaves from converting solely to gain freedom. Three years later the colony ruled that any non-Christian servant arriving in Virginia by ship was subject to lifetime enslavement. Since Africans were the only non-Christians traveling to the New World, the law was specifically aimed at them. By the 1700s slavery was an established institution in the colonies, and statutes regulating its practices were no longer oblique. In 1705 the Virginia General Assembly declared: "All Negro, mulatto and Indian slaves shall be held, taken, and adjudged to be real estate, in the same category as livestock and household furniture, wagons, and goods."

A steady and prosperous slave trade from the west coast of Africa to the east coast of America flourished until 1807, when the slave trade ended. During this time, sadly, tribal warfare in Africa made the job easier for the White slave merchants, who traded guns, ammunition, and powder for precious human bounty. Males and females were tightly packed into ships, without regard for tribal differences, for the long and perilous sea journey. Lack of sanitation, proper nourishment, and exercise took their toll on the high seas. The voyage was particularly gruesome for females, who were frequently raped by White sailors and sometimes became pregnant along the way. For those who survived the middle passage, the cruelties of slavery awaited. Sold at auction and separated from their loved ones, most Africans ended up on southern farms or plantations to work as field hands or house servants.

There were never enough slaves to satisfy the demand, and throughout the seventeenth and eighteenth centuries White landowners also relied on indentured servants to help clear the land and plant crops. Indentured servitude was a common practice in Europe, and an estimated 80 percent of the English immigrants who came to America during its early years paid for their passage with four to seven years of faithful labor for temporary owners. Most indentured servants were members of the lower class who came to the New World to start life anew; some, however, were convicted criminals and prostitutes who were banished to America as punishment.

In colonial America, especially in the area around Chesapeake Bay, White indentured servants and Black slaves frequently worked side by side on large plantations. Because they shared the same lifestyles, privileges, and restrictions, they became friends and sometimes lovers.

A shortage of women, both African and European, contributed to the widespread mixing of races in early America. Among Africans there were at least three men for every two women, and among Whites men outnumbered women by as many as three or four to one, especially in the South. Given this gender imbalance, as well as the harsh realities of frontier life, the selection of a mate tended to be more pragmatic than romantic. Offers of marriage were often made on the basis of opportunity and ability to protect and procreate. Free White men married African slaves, sometimes the only women they knew, and White female servants accepted the proposals of Black men, although this interracial pattern met with more resistance and was far less common.

African males also turned to Indian women for love and marriage, especially when the already short supply of African females was further drained by marriages to White men. Although the natives initially feared the Black man and called him "Manitto," a word meaning both God and Devil, the two groups eventually came to regard each other as equals.

Colonial Whites tended to ignore the sexual affairs of Indians and Blacks. Both groups were considered of low status, and were left alone as long as they did not interfere with daily life in the colonies. Meanwhile, Indians and Africans were consolidating their hatred of the White man. Africans were usually spared when Indians executed their revenge on White settlements; in the Virginia massacre of 1622, not a single one of more than twenty slaves was harmed by the Indians. Later, Indians often provided runaway slaves with a safe refuge, and sometimes these slaves stayed to raise families within the tribe. In some cases, so much interracial mixing occurred that entire Indian tribes were genetically absorbed into the Black population. Anthropologists calculate that as many as one-fourth of all Blacks in America have some Indian ancestry—a convincing estimate if one examines the features and skin color of many African Americans today.

Although the race mixing of Indians and Africans was of little interest to the colonial Whites, the rapid proliferation of White-Black race mixing was causing them great alarm. For slavery to gain moral acceptance, it was essential to keep the races apart. White leaders knew that if sexual relations with Africans continued unchecked, ethical questions about slavery would surely follow. As early as 1622, a little more than two years after the first Africans had arrived, Virginia legislators passed the earliest antimiscegenation statutes. Most of these laws implied that Africans were a lower life form than Europeans; they proclaimed that sexual union between Whites and Blacks was twice as evil as fornication between two Whites, and that sex with Negroes was equivalent to bestiality.

Despite such strong public condemnation, colonial males and females, White and Black, continued to fall in love and intermarry. Historical records document complaints by White masters when this happened among slaves and servants. In 1720, Richard Tilghman of Philadelphia filed a protest when his mulatto slave, Richard Moslon, escaped with a White woman, and in 1747 a White servant named Ann Wainwright, of New Castle County, reportedly ran off with a Negro man. Concern was greatest when, as in these two cases, the interracial relationship involved a White woman and a Black man There were far too few White females in the colonies for White authorities to tolerate their being sexually active with Black men, and lawmakers meted out stern punishments for such transgressions. In Maryland, for example, a White female servant who had sex with a Black male slave was subject to a lifetime of enslavement. Unfortunately for many poor English women, this law had the peculiar effect of instigating White owners to encourage their male slaves to rape their White servants so that these women, too, would become slave property.

The delicate matter of a White master's fornication with his female slaves also required attention. Although the topic was one that most Whites would rather have avoided, the practice was common enough for the resulting mulatto children to become a problem in the colonies. The central question for colonial lawmakers to settle was whether mixed-breed offspring should have the free status of the White father or the slave status of the Black mother. Virginia's legislators found a solution that worked to their advantage. Departing from traditional English law, in which the status of the child was always determined by that of the father, the colonists voted in 1662 that children in Virginia would have the same status as the mother. Not exactly a victory for women's rights, this statute allowed, even encouraged, owners to increase slaveholdings through sexual misconduct. The law also dashed slave women's hopes that their mulatto offspring might go free.

Not all mulatto offspring in the early years of America were subject to slavery, though. Children born of free Colored parents were free, as were those born of free Colored mothers and slave fathers. In addition, mulattoes born of White females and Black slave fathers lived free, as did most children of mixed Negro and Indian parentage.

As the number of free colonial mulattoes grew exponentially, they were increasingly treated as outcasts, visible reminders of the state's failure to keep the races apart. Neither fully White nor Negro, mulattoes lay outside the social order. Certain rights, like holding property, running for office, and voting, were reserved exclusively for Whites and denied to Negroes. Free mulattoes required legal definition, preferably in a way that would maintain the status quo. How they came to be classified did much to create the color-caste system that lingers in America today.

In the upper South, including Virginia and Maryland, legislators decided that any person with even a drop of Black blood would have the same legal status as a pure African. This early statute became the basis of today's "one-drop rule" (also called the one-drop theory) of racial identity, which has its origin in racist concern about the contamination of the White gene pool; no matter how White looking or White acting someone of mixed ancestry is or how little Blackness is in a person's genetic makeup, that person is considered Black. Even when part of an individual's genetic lineage is Indian, he or she is usually considered Black.

By the early 1700s this curiously inclusive definition of Negroes was firmly entrenched in the upper South. The one-drop rule also spread to the North, where it was widely accepted even after industrialization made slavery unnecessary, and well into the early 1800s, when slavery was no longer legal in the North. By then mulattoes shared the bottom rung of the social hierarchy with unmixed Negroes and superficial differences between the two mattered little.

This was not the case farther south. In the region below North

Carolina race mixing occurred later in the nation's history and tended to follow a different pattern. The continuing shortage of European women in sparsely populated agricultural areas led many White plantation owners to become not only sexually but also emotionally involved with their Black female slaves and attached to the children of those relationships. Mulattoes in the deep South were typically not the descendants of lower-class servants, but often the loved progeny of the finest families. Early on, some plantation owners freed their mulatto sons and daughters, who were sometimes the only children they had, and helped them get a start in business or trade or in farming. Some even provided them with slaves of their own. White legislators, some of whom had themselves fathered such children, were inclined to be more liberal regarding the legal status of mulattoes. As a result, mulattoes of the deep South attained the status of a separate Colored class. In some colonies, including South Carolina, mulattoes who were "proper acting," a quality determined by their wealth and education, could even apply for legal standing as "White." Those with light-enough skin and European features commonly got around the law by simply passing as White.

A three-tiered social system thus evolved in the lower South, with mulattoes serving as a buffer class between Whites and Blacks. Members of the White elite found advantages in this arrangement. Necessary business transactions between the races could be conducted through mulattoes, whose presence reduced racial tensions, especially in areas where Negroes outnumbered Whites.

Prior to the Revolutionary War the free mulatto population of the deep South was quite small, but it grew after the war. Ironically, the British, in seeking to defeat America's drive for independence, guaranteed freedom to any slave who escaped and joined their forces. Some slaves took advantage of the offer and remained free when the British surrendered. Other Negroes served in the Continental Army, because masters who were drafted were allowed to send slaves as substitutes. Still other slaves took advantage of the wartime confusion to escape and hide among free Blacks. And, finally, a few owners, caught up in the patriotic spirit, freed all their slaves when America declared its independence from England.

The resulting flood of manumitted and escaped Negroes darkened the free Black community. Accustomed by now to their unique status as a buffer class, the privileged mulattoes worried that Whites would now associate them with these poorer, darker-skinned new arrivals. Social distinctions within the Colored community were increasingly made on the basis of skin color and the length of time a person had been free. Mulattoes living free in Charleston, South Carolina, and other cities intermingled and intermarried only with each other, actively discriminating against those who were dark.

Literature attests to the unique and curious status of the mulatto elite in the deep South. In *Pride of Family,* author Carole Ione discovers the diary of her great-grandmother, Frances (Frank) Anne Rollin, who lived in Charleston before and after the Civil War. Ione also finds a biography Frank wrote of Martin Delany, an early abolitionist and civil-rights activist. In the Delany biography Frank describes the situation of the free Colored people of Charleston during the 1840s.

They were an intermediate class in all the slave states, standing between the whites and the bondmen, known as the free colored; debarred from enjoying the privileges of the one, but superior in condition to the other, more, however, by sufferance than by actual law. They were subject to the machinations and jealousies of the non-slaveholders, whom they rivaled in mechanical skill and trade. . . . [Yet] they were excluded from the more liberal and learned professions. . . . [And] there were influences always at work to deprive them of the fruits of their labor, either openly or covertly.

Class distinctions made on the basis of color were also common among the Creoles, who were of French, Spanish, and African descent. When revolutions rocked the West Indies in the 1790s, a wave of Creoles—also called Creoles of Color or Black Creoles, depending on their Black ancestry—fled to America, settling predominantly in Charleston and lower Louisiana. They came mostly from Haiti and Santo Domingo (formerly Saint-Dominique), and they brought with them their French Catholic culture, still evident in New Orleans today. A few were wealthy, having benefited, like the mulattoes of the old South, from being members of a buffer class separating masters and slaves in the West Indies.

The color-conscious Creoles quickly rose to positions of power and influence within the Colored community, and before long being Creole in itself garnered respect. While many Negroes aspired to the social standing of the Creoles, others rejected their snobbish ways. In Charles Johnson's novel *Middle Passage,* a recently freed slave in New Orleans reacts strongly to a suggestion by his dark-skinned girl-friend from the North that he try to act more like a Creole.

> It was what you heard all your blessed life from black elders
> and church women in flowered gowns: Don't be common.
> Comb your hair. Be a credit to the Race. Strive, like the Cre-
> oles, for respectability. Class. It made my insides clench.

Yet it was difficult to emulate—much less penetrate—the Creole population. Their marriages were arranged so that the "purity" of the bloodline could be maintained. To this day, many Creoles see themselves as separate from other Blacks in America. In general, they resist the one-drop rule of racial identity, preferring a three-tiered system of racial classification in which they place themselves well above others of African descent.

Before the Civil War, free persons of color in the South were an unusual and often elite group. Some became leaders of the Black community, often with the sponsorship of a White ancestor. Throughout the era of slavery there were occasional masters who risked arrest by providing for the education of their mixed offspring or by arranging for them to escape when they were old enough. Some of these own-ers sent their mulatto children abroad, to the finest schools in Europe, and on their return they became some of the earliest Black educators, doctors, and lawyers in America.

While before the Civil War the majority of those of African de-scent living free in the South were mulatto, most mulattoes of that era and region remained enslaved. Approximately 10 percent of the more than 400,000 slaves in the South before 1860 had some degree of White blood. Yet since mulattoes brought the highest prices on the slave market, even among slaves those with the lightest skin had the highest status, especially on the larger plantations.

Coveted indoor assignments, including artisan, driver, valet, seamstress, cook, and housekeeper, were nearly always reserved for mulattoes, while the physically grueling field work was typically left to slaves who were dark skinned. Masters considered mulattoes more intelligent and capable than pure Africans, who in turn were thought to be stronger and better able to tolerate the hot sun. As color increasingly divided the slave community, frictions developed in the cabins. Light-skinned slaves returning home from their days in the "big house" imitated the genteel ways of upper-class white families, and the mulatto offspring of the master often flaunted their education. Many field hands both envied and resented the house servants. Yet working in daily close proximity to a White master had its own risks, especially if one was female.

Rape was a fact of life on the plantations. At any time and in any place, female slaves were subject to the drunken or abusive sexual advances of a master, an overseer, a neighbor, or a master's son. Few Black women reached the age of sixteen without having been molested by a White male. The African women's dark skin seemed to have a profound effect on the White man's psyche, and many White men longed to escape the suffocating effects of a Christian ethic that equated sex with sin. Southern White males, nursed at a Black servant's bosom as infants, often experienced their first real sexual pleasure as men in the arms of Black women. They fantasized about these women's "animalistic" nature, as the eighteenth-century poem at the beginning of this chapter shows.

In some parts of the South mulattoes were actually bred and sold for huge profit on the female slave market. Pretty quadroons (one-quarter Black) and exotic octoroons (one-eighth Black) were in particularly high demand. Light-skinned beauties, called "fancy girls," were auctioned at "quadroon balls" held regularly in New Orleans and Charleston. A respectable White gentleman might buy a concubine, and when he tired of her, six months or so later, he might get himself another one. If he found one he liked, he might keep her for life.

Some Whites lived openly with their Black female mistresses. One southerner, a man named William Adams, stipulated in his will that his Black concubine, Nancy, be set free upon his death and awarded a portion of his property. He even left money for the children he had fathered by her. Adams's White son was outraged, however, and successfully challenged the will in court. The judge declared Nancy and all of her children to be part of the son's estate.

The most famous and controversial case of a "White gentleman" keeping a mulatto concubine was Thomas Jefferson, author of the Declaration of Independence and third president of the United States. While hard proof of the affair is lacking, the circumstantial evidence is compelling.

In 1772, Thomas Jefferson married a widow named Martha (Wayles) Skelton, the daughter of John Wayles, a prosperous local plantation owner. Martha's father, a widower, kept a beautiful mulatto concubine named Betty Hemings. Shortly after Thomas and Martha's marriage the concubine gave birth to a daughter, Sally, who thus became Martha's illegitimate half sister. John Wayles died not long after Sally's birth, and Martha inherited 40,000 acres of land and 135 slaves, including Betty and Sally Hemings.

Jefferson's marriage to Martha was by all indications a happy one. She bore him six children, although only two survived to adulthood. But she suffered from poor health and had frequent miscarriages, and she died at the age of thirty-three, after ten years of marriage. At the time, Sally was nine years old and serving as Martha's personal servant. Jefferson was extremely distraught over his wife's death and turned to public service to escape his depression. He spent two years as a delegate to the Continental Congress and then, in 1784, he left for Europe, taking his two older children with him. After a year in London, he moved to Paris, where he served nearly four years as minister to France.

While in Paris Jefferson received more tragic news from home: his second youngest child had died. Grief stricken at losing yet another family member, he sent for his youngest daughter, Polly. The older slave who was supposed to accompany Polly on the long journey to Europe took ill, and a hurried decision was made to send Sally instead. Sally, who was now fourteen years old and showing unmistakable signs of becoming a woman, was a beauty. Jefferson's heart must have skipped a beat at his first sight of her—she bore an uncanny resemblance to his departed wife.

Some historians believe that Jefferson began an affair with Sally Hemings almost immediately after her arrival in Paris. One possible indication of a growing obsession with her can be found in his journal. Prior to her arrival in Paris, Jefferson used the word "mulatto" only once in forty-eight pages, but shortly afterward "mulatto" appeared eight times in fewer than twenty-five pages. He described even the countryside of Holland as "mulatto," a curious adjective for the highly literate Jefferson to employ.

When he was getting ready to return to America in 1789, Sally announced that she was pregnant, presumably with his child. At that point she was forced to decide whether to accompany Jefferson back to America or to stay abroad. She would be free as long as she lived in France, but if she returned to America she would return to slavery. Jefferson allegedly persuaded her with promises of material wealth and the guaranteed freedom of her unborn child.

In 1801, Jefferson was sworn in as the third president of the United States. Some believe that he and Sally were still lovers, more than ten years after their return from Paris. She continued to live at Monticello, his Charlottesville estate, and over the years she bore five more light-skinned children. Whether Jefferson fathered any or all of them remains unknown, and some biographers now think that the father of Sally Hemings's mulatto children was one of Jefferson's nephews, not Jefferson himself. But then why did Jefferson's will allow only Sally's children, of all the slaves on his plantation, to go north to freedom?

American scholars have largely ignored the possibility that Thomas Jefferson kept a mulatto concubine. Perhaps they found it hard to believe that the same person who wrote "all men are created equal" not only owned slaves but fathered children by one of them. It was several decades after Jefferson's death before any of the evidence was examined, and by then much of it had been lost or destroyed.

Although a few mulatto slaves, including Sally Hemings and some of the "fancy girls," may have led richer and more comfortable lives as a result of their concubinage, a much greater number of female slaves suffered horribly from constant and brutal sexual exploitation. Physical and psychic wounds were inflicted on these Black women from which many never recovered.

Some of the most sadistic behavior inflicted on female house servants was at the hands of White wives in retaliation for their husbands' affairs. Suspiciously White-looking mulatto children were particularly vulnerable targets for punishment, as reflected in Margaret Walker's Civil War novel *Jubilee*. The protagonist of the story is a house servant named Vyry, a mulatto daughter of the master, who closely resembles her White siblings and as a result must endure the wrath of Big Missy, the master's wife. In the following excerpt, a young Vyry has forgotten to remove Big Missy's chamber pot.

The morning with fear of the whipping she learned she was going to get she stood before Big Missy, who was standing in the doorway of the kitchen and holding the pot of stale pee in her hand. Instead of whipping her, she threw the acrid contents of the pot in Vyry's face and said, "There, you lazy nigger, that'll teach you to keep your mind on what you're doing. Don't let me have to tell you another time about this pot or I'll half kill you, do you hear me?"

White wives also tended to callously disregard the emotional needs of their female slaves, as set forth in Harriet Jacobs's autobiographical *Incidents in the Life of a Slave Girl*.

Moreover, my mistress, like many others, seemed to think that slaves had no right to any family ties of their own; that they were created merely to wait upon the family of the mistress. I once heard her abuse a young slave girl, who told her that a colored man wanted to make her his wife. "I will have you peeled and pickled, my lady," said she, "if I ever hear you mention that subject again. Do you suppose that I will have you tending *my* children with the children of that nigger?"

There were some White women, however, who simply resigned themselves to the fact that the men they had married were unfaithful. And a few even implored their female slaves to become sexually involved with their wayward husbands—a Black lover would at least be less threatening than a White one.

While the wives and daughters of many slave owners led lives almost as limited as those of their slaves, some had lovers of their own in the slave cabin. While little has been written about White women crossing the color line for sexual excitement, there were those who did so regularly—a few even abandoned their husbands for dark-skinned men. Some White women even flaunted such affairs, talking openly about the Negro male's sexual prowess. In 1837, a Kentucky minister named John Rankin disclosed that the daughters of some of the finest White families had had affairs with their fathers' male slaves. Some White women also became involved with free men of color. One African man who lived in Louisiana and was described as having a "body of Hercules and with eyes as black as the moonless nights of Africa" kept two White concubines who produced a total of nineteen mulatto children.

White women's mulatto children disrupted the patriarchy, however. Mulattoes in the slave quarters were an economic asset, in the form of slave property, but a racially mixed child in the "big house" created havoc and shame. Because of the one-drop rule the child was considered Black, but because the law defined a child's status as that of its mother, the child was also free. If the woman was married, her husband almost always filed for divorce. If she was single, her options were few: send the child away, usually north, to be reared by someone else; give it to a local slave family; leave her White family and join the Black community; or move to the frontier and raise the child there.

Black men who were sexually involved with White women risked far more, however. If caught, they could be whipped, castrated, or murdered for defiling "the sanctity of white womanhood." The Black man who so much as looked at a White female risked a spontaneous lynching, often initiated by the same White men who were indulging their sexual urges with Black women. The Black man's dark skin became the sign of a dangerous and potent sexuality, and the darker the skin, the greater the threat to White manhood. Meanwhile, Black men felt symbolically castrated by their inability to stop the White master from raping their women, and White masters frequently used the threat of rape as a weapon of terror against the entire slave community.

As the South came under increasing attack from the North for its refusal to end slavery, these racial and sexual tensions mounted. The former alliance between free mulattoes and Whites weakened, and in the deep South support for the three-tier system of racial classification eroded. State after state moved in the direction of a two-class society racially divided by the one-drop rule.

By the time of the Civil War, sexual relations between Whites and Blacks were becoming less common in the South, and the social upheaval and economic devastation brought on by the war did nothing to reverse the trend. Even after the war, when there was a shortage of White men, few White women turned to Black men as lovers or husbands. Vigilante groups like the Ku Klux Klan had risen up, determined to keep the races apart.

Yet even if Whites and Blacks could be kept from ever intermingling again, "White genes" would continue to be disseminated through the Black community via the marriage of mulattoes to unmixed Blacks. Only a few Negro groups living in the most isolated rural areas, like the Angolan Blacks near the coast of South Carolina, would escape the dilution of their African genes. More than two centuries of race mixing between masters, slaves, and lovers, both White and Indian, had already produced a population of Negroes more racially mixed than pure.

The resulting rainbow of skin colors, however, would hardly be distributed randomly across the socioeconomic spectrum. The preferential treatment of mulattoes by Whites had laid the groundwork for a pattern of color classism in Black America.

2. The Color Gap in Power and Privilege

Whiter and whiter, every generation. The nearer white you are the more
white people will respect you. Therefore all light Negroes marry light Negroes.
Continue to do so generation after generation, and eventually white people
will accept this racially bastard aristocracy, thus enabling those Negroes
who really matter to escape the social and economic inferiority of the
American Negro.
—WALLACE THURMAN,
  The Blacker the Berry

After the Civil War the mulatto elite no longer had the distinction
of freedom to separate them from the dark-skinned masses. Many
mulattoes, disenfranchised by the war effort, suffered not only from
the loss of property, business, and wealth but also from the backlash
of White Southerners, some of whom had previously supported them.
To preserve their status this colored elite began to segregate themselves into a separate community. In the process they actively discriminated against their darker-skinned brethren. In many ways, the
mulatto elite acted no differently than any other upper-class group
attempting to secure its status. Rich White people attend preppie
schools, form exclusive business associations, and join fancy country
clubs in order to mingle and mate with the "right" kind. Light-skinned
Blacks were simply doing the same. In another sense, however, the
mulattoes' behavior differed in that a single visible attribute, skin
color, determined who would be accepted. The elitism that had begun
before the Civil War became further entrenched after it, and still remains evident today in the color gap in power and privilege that divides the Black community.

Mulatto elite social clubs like the Bon Ton Society of Washington, D.C., and the Blue Vein Society of Nashville were formed during Reconstruction, when southern cities were flooded with the "sot-free," Negroes freed by the Emancipation Proclamation. The elite group of those who had been free before the war, in many case for generations, called themselves the "bona fide" free and reacted to the upheaval by forming exclusive social clubs based on color and class, which provided an effective way to maintain the old hierarchy. Membership was considered an honor, and the "blue veiners" and "bon tonners" were thought to have the finest of bloodlines. In practice, however, admission to a blue vein society depended not on family background but on skin color. An applicant had to be fair enough for the spidery network of purplish veins at the wrist to be visible to a panel of expert judges. Access to certain vacation resorts, like Highland Beach on Chesapeake Bay, was even said to be restricted to blue-vein members.

Many Negroes, mulatto and otherwise, thought the blue veiners ridiculous and called their clubs blue "vain" societies. Others, like the writer Wallace Thurman, were alarmed by the organizations' political agenda. The fictitious blue vein society is the quoted at the beginning of this chapter was an attempt by Thurman to call attention to the true nature of these clubs.

Not until after the Black Renaissance of the 1920s did the influence and prevalence of the mulatto social clubs weaken, although snobbish attitudes about skin color and class persisted. To this day exclusive Black social clubs like Jack & Jill and Links have a significant majority of light-skinned members. Many churches, schools, sororities, fraternities, businesses, and even neighborhoods are also reputed to be partial to light-skinned Blacks.

Virtually every major urban center across the country has a section where predominantly light-skinned Blacks reside. In Philadelphia, mulattoes live in areas unofficially called "lighty brighty" and "banana block." In Chicago, the Black bourgeoisie can be found in Chatham and East Hyde Park, and in New York, certain sections of Harlem remain reserved for descendants of the light-skinned mulatto elite.

Although most Americans think of Harlem as a wasteland of drugs and crime, two small areas prevail as reminders of what the neighborhood once was. Strivers Row, located between West 138th and West 139th streets and Seventh and Eighth avenues, was originally occupied by wealthy White families who quickly vacated when Blacks began to "invade" Harlem in 1918. Light-skinned doctors, lawyers, ministers, journalists, teachers, and other professionals, haughtily known as the "Elite of African Descent," were only too happy to take up residence in the beautiful brownstone houses the fleeing Whites left behind. During the roaring twenties Strivers Row was *the* place to live for New York's mulatto socialites. Harlem Congressman Adam Clayton Powell, Sr., wrote of living there in the 1940s, when the neighborhood was still very much in vogue.

> . . . in Strivers Row . . . were the dowagers of Harlem's society. These queenly, sometimes portly, and nearly always light-skinned Czarinas presided over the Harlem upper class. . . . There was an open door for all who were light-skinned and for most of those of the professional group. The entire pattern of society was white. . . . [And] if invited Harlemites brought with them [to a social function] their dark-skinned friends, they were shunned and sometimes pointedly asked to leave.

Another exclusive neighborhood is nearby Sugar Hill, so-called because the people who live there are said to lead such a "sweet" life. The "Hill" slopes from West 145th to West 155th streets between Edgecombe and Amsterdam avenues and overlooks the "Valley," where, with the exception of Strivers Row, the less-fortunate Harlemites reside. In the 1920s light-skinned Blacks with money, talent, social prominence, and intellectual distinction migrated to the high-rent white stone apartment houses of the "Hill." The fourteen-story building at 409 Edgecombe became a particular address of choice. It remains tony today, and one past occupant who does not speak for others in the building believes that "unless you are of light skin color, you are not welcome" as a tenant. According to this source, when the tenants of 409 are called on their color classism, as they often are, they tend to respond in a tone of innocent sarcasm, *"Not* 409!'

Historically, there have been certain Black churches that were highly color conscious as well. Churches have generally played a more vital role in the lives of Blacks than in those of Whites. The sociologist W. E. B. DuBois once referred to the church as "the social center of Negro life." Thus, like members of social clubs, churchgoers have tended to congregate by color and class.

The earliest church in America established exclusively for Negroes was the African Methodist Episcopal Church (AME), founded in 1793 in Philadelphia. By 1870, with color increasingly dividing the Black community, the lighter-skinned worshipers split off to form their own denomination, called the Colored Methodist Episcopal (the "C" in CME was changed in 1954 to stand for Christian). Fair-skinned bishops were the rule in the CME, a pattern that prompted a prominent Black newspaper editor to write, in 1910, "there is now but one of the dark hue, all the others being mulattoes, quadroons or octoroons."

At the turn of the century, Black families wishing to join a color-conscious congregation might first be required to pass the paper-bag, the door, or the comb test. The paper-bag test involved placing an arm inside a brown paper bag, and only if the skin on the arm was lighter than the color of the bag would a prospective member be invited to attend church services. Other churches painted their doors a light shade of brown, and anyone whose skin was darker than the door was politely invited to seek religious services elsewhere. And in still other "houses of worship" throughout Virginia and in such cities as Philadelphia and New Orleans, a fine-toothed comb was hung on a rope near the front entrance. If one's hair was too nappy and snagged in the comb, entry was denied.

Although such qualifying tests for church membership have long since disappeared, the congregations of certain Black society churches continue to be noticeably lighter than others. Inside these churches one hears none of the loud gospel singing, hand clapping, or foot stomping stereotypically associated with Black churches. In Atlanta, the locals joke that no one can join the First Congregational Church unless his or her skin is as light as the lightest faces in the stained-glass windows. Like St. Stephen's Episcopal Church in Savannah,

First Congregational was often referred to as a blue vein, or b.v., church.

Perhaps the most insidious form of color discrimination was found at the Black preparatory schools and colleges established by and for the mulatto elite. Dark-skinned Blacks were often denied admission regardless of their academic qualifications. At the Palmer Institute in Sedalia, North Carolina, in the early years of the twentieth century, one of the more prestigious Black preparatory schools in the country, headmistress Dr. Charlotte Hawkins Brown even avoided using the terms Black or Colored in discussions with her mostly light-skinned, fine-featured students. Instead she said "one of us" or "our kind." And although White features might signal illegitimacy, Dr. Brown apparently thought it was not a bad thing to have a White ancestor or two somewhere back in the family tree. A similar attitude prevailed in New Orleans at the St. Mary's Academy for Young Ladies of Color, a finishing school for the daughters of well-to-do Creoles. Dark-skinned students who managed to get accepted at these schools were often ostracized. At the legendary M Street High School (later renamed Dunbar) in Washington, D.C., a graduate of 1905 claimed that while a dark-skinned youth might receive a good education there, the children of the old mulatto families would never accept him as a social equal. These schoolday social patterns were extremely important, since friendships formed early in life were often the basis for useful political and business contacts later on.

Cliquish social circles and biased admissions policies were also common at many of the historic Black colleges and universities established in the nineteenth century, including Wilberforce in Ohio (1856), Howard in Washington, D.C. (1867), Fisk University in Nashville (1866), Atlanta University in Georgia (1865), Morgan (today Morgan State) in Baltimore (1867), Hampton Institute (today Hampton University) in Virginia (1868), and Spelman Women's College in Atlanta (1881). At some of the most prestigious of the schools, including Spelman, applicants were allegedly required to pass a color test before being admitted.

A principal mission of these schools was to groom mulattoes in the genteel mores of the bourgeoisie; students received a primarily liberal arts education. Many academic administrators considered it a waste of time to train dark-skinned Negroes for paths in life that would be closed to them, and as recently as 1916 it was estimated that 80 percent of the students of these Black colleges were light skinned and of mixed ancestry.

Denied a liberal arts education, dark-skinned students began turning to schools like Tuskegee Institute of Alabama, founded in 1881 by Booker T. Washington. Tuskegee offered all Black students a strictly vocational curriculum of "industrial education" because Washington thought that Negroes, particularly those who were not members of the aristocracy, should concentrate their energies on becoming skilled workers.

Another college president who rejected a liberal arts education in favor of vocational training was Mary McLeod Bethune, a woman of blue-black coloring who established the Bethune-Cookman College of Daytona, Florida, in 1927. Her institution, originally called the Daytona School for Girls, was founded expressly for "Black girls," not the fair-skinned daughters of doctors, lawyers, and clergymen who attended Palmer. Bethune students took a curriculum of basic skills, including home economics, cooking, and even housekeeping, so that upon graduation they would be fully prepared to do real work in the real world.

Although Washington was himself a mulatto, advocates of industrial education were often darker-skinned while proponents of liberal arts studies tended to be members of the mulatto elite. (When Washington died in 1915, a dark-skinned Black man, Robert Russa Moten, was named to succeed him as president of Tuskegee.) The separate educational paths taken by light-skinned mulattoes and dark-skinned Negroes at the turn of the century further divided the Black community. Evidence began to mount that an industrial education did nothing more than channel dark-skinned Blacks into low-paying menial work.

Does skin color still affect educational and occupational opportunities for African-American college students today? In the late 1980s, Ronald Hall questioned Black students from comparable social and educational backgrounds attending a predominantly Black university in the South about their career plans. He found a strong correlation between skin color and occupational goals: the light-skinned students aimed for far more prestigious jobs than their darker-skinned peers.

Students on Black college campuses also claim that skin color affects their social opportunities, especially within the Greek system. Some maintain that membership in the more exclusive organizations still depends largely on having the right hair texture and skin color. However, many "Greeks" dispute this claim, arguing that skin color has never been a factor distinguishing Black fraternities and sororities, since most were founded at the turn of the century when the vast majority of students were mulatto. Others confess that when students from more varied backgrounds started attending college, color did start to become a factor in the hierarchy of Greek organizations: the more elite the fraternity or sorority, the lighter-skinned its members. The highly regarded Alpha Kappa Alpha sorority and Kappa Alpha Psi fraternity must still contend with reputations for being partial toward Blacks with light skin and "good" hair.

In the past, even guests of student members at color elite organizations were subject to the paper-bag tests. From the 1920s well into the 1960s "color tax" parties were common in Black fraternities— the darker a brother's date, the higher the tax he had to pay at the door. While most students deny that there is any such outright color prejudice today, nonetheless those of similar shading and features do seem to gravitate together, as Spike Lee showed in his film *School Daze*.

Historically, Black business organizations discriminated on the basis of skin color as well, particularly in cities like Charleston and New Orleans where relatively large populations of mulattoes lived free before emancipation. In Charleston, the Brown Fellowship Society was established in 1790 by free people of color to facilitate business contacts among Negroes, but membership was restricted to those whose skin was light to medium brown. (Ambitious darker-skinned Black men were left to form their own business organization, the Society of Free Dark Men.) Clubs and organizations like these kept mulattoes a distinct class apart from the rest of the Black community. By socializing only with each other, they produced generations of light-skinned Blacks—an aristocracy whose money and ancestral portraits often went back to great-great-grandparents who were free before the Civil War.

By the turn of the century, this mulatto elite had clearly emerged as the intellectual and political leaders of the Black community. The visibility and power of this select group was never more clear than when a volume of essays devoted to various aspects of the "American Negro problem" was published by the Pott Company in 1903. Contemporary Black intellectuals were invited to make scholarly contributions; all but one of the seven were mulatto. An essay by W. E. B. DuBois called on the Negro community to "produce a college-educated class whose mission would be to serve and guide the progress of the masses." Among those DuBois designated to help lead the way were twenty-one men and two women, all but one of whom were mulatto. This list of leaders, popularly known as the "Talented Tenth" (a reference to the "top" 10 percent of the Negro population), included:

Ira Aldridge	Negro actor	mulatto
Benjamin Banneker	Invented clock	mulatto
B. K. Bruce	Politician	mulatto
Paul Cuffe	Activist	mulatto
Frederick Douglass	Antislavery activist	mulatto
James Durham	Practiced medicine	mulatto
R. B. Elliot	Politician	mulatto
H. H. Garnett	Preacher	mulatto
R. T. Greener	Politician	mulatto
Lemuel Haynes	Preacher	mulatto
John Langston	Politician	mulatto
D. A. Payne	Bishop of A.M. church	mulatto
J. W. C. Pennington	Underground railroad	mulatto
Phyllis Wheatley Peters	Writer	black
Robert Purvis	Underground railroad	mulatto
J. B. Russworm	Governor of Liberia	mulatto
McCune Smith	Physician/druggist	mulatto
Sojourner Truth	Underground Railroad	mulatto

David Walker	Agitator	mulatto
B. T. Washington	Principal at Tuskegee	mulatto
Bert Williams	Comedian	mulatto

Despite being named as one of the "upper tens," the educator Booker T. Washington was among those who rejected DuBois's premise that a few shining examples of successful, well-educated Blacks at the top would in any way help the average Black person at the bottom.

DuBois and Washington may have differed in their political views, but they both had light skin and Caucasian features. Washington had reddish hair and gray eyes; DuBois, with his mixture of French, Dutch, and African blood, was so light that some said he could easily have passed as White. As DuBois's "Talented Tenth" list made abundantly clear, possessing a degree of mixed ancestry was a definite asset when it came to being considered a voice for the Negro race.

Frederick Douglass, for example, was one of the earliest Negro leaders in the United States. Born in 1817, the son of a White Maryland slaveholder and a slave woman, Douglass was raised as a slave. In 1838, however, he escaped north to freedom, and within two years he had become known as a stunning lecturer as well as a leading abolitionist. By the end of his life Douglass had been a newspaper editor, the president of the Freedman's Bank, the U.S. minister to Haiti, and a U.S. marshal for the District of Columbia.

Robert Purvis, the son of a free mulatto woman and a wealthy Charleston merchant, was another important early Black leader. Sent north to be educated at Amherst College in Massachusetts, he later became one of the founders of the American Anti-Slavery Society. And James Augustine Healy, the son of a mulatto slave and an Irish planter, was also educated in the North and then went abroad, where he was eventually ordained as a priest at Notre Dame Cathedral in Paris. When he returned to the United States he served in Portland, Maine, as this country's first Black bishop. From 1873 to 1882 he was president of Georgetown University, and is considered its second founder.

Healy must have felt very much at home in the District of Columbia, one of the hubs of mulatto society. During Reconstruction all but three of the twenty Black congressmen and two Black senators serving in Washington were mulatto. By virtue of their color, this unique group had access not only to education but also, in some cases, to the wealth of a White ancestor.

Yet there were exceptions to the rule. Some dark-skinned Blacks also rose to positions of power and leadership. In the nineteenth century, Jonathan Wright of Pennsylvania became one of the three justices of the state Supreme Court, serving between 1870 and 1877; in South Carolina, Beverly Nash and William Whipper, both dark-skinned members of the 1868 constitutional convention, went on to become leading state legislators.

Meanwhile, Marcus Garvey became the apostle of pure Blackness. Born in Jamaica, Garvey moved to Harlem and started his infamous "back to Africa" movement. His travel plans included the establishment of a colony of transplanted Afro-Americans in Liberia, from which a power base could be built to force White imperialists off the African continent. He founded the Universal Negro Improvement Association and published a newspaper called the *Negro World* as means of promoting his back-to-Africa campaign.

In Garvey's worldview, unadulterated Blackness was equivalent to spotless morality, a position that outraged members of the mulatto elite. When Garvey ridiculed DuBois for trying to "be everything else but a Negro," DuBois fired back by calling Garvey "fat, Black, and ugly." Garvey may have alienated mulattoes, but his movement uplifted the spirits of many beleaguered dark-skinned Black Americans, giving them a renewed sense of heritage, destiny, and pride. In the end, though, Garvey's crusade was bound to fail. By the turn of the century only a minority of American Negroes could claim a pure Black ancestry, and Garvey's political message was at odds with the power brokers of his own community—the lighter-skinned aristocracy.

Throughout the twentieth century most of the leaders of the Black community have been extraordinarily light skinned. The Reverend Adam Clayton Powell, Jr., with his blue eyes, aquiline features, almost blond hair, and old family background, was typical of this group.

During the 1930s he was the pastor of the Abyssinian Baptist Church in Harlem and used his pulpit to create a political base that won him election to the New York city council and later to the U.S. House of Representatives. As a congressman, he was not afraid to attack the White power structure, and he lobbied hard for the passage of anti-discrimination legislation.

Anthropologists have estimated that the blue-eyed, blond-haired, white-skinned Walter White was no more than one sixty-fourth Black in his racial makeup, yet he identified himself as Black and did much to champion Negro causes. He served as president of the National Association for the Advancement of Colored People (NAACP) from 1931 to 1955, yet he was so White looking that he was able to pass while personally investigating lynchings in the South. Another light-skinned Black who rose to an impressive position of leadership was A. Philip Randolph. He was raised in Florida, in a family that could have passed, but his parents chose instead to teach him moral outrage about the existence of racism. His early experiences served him well, and after he moved to New York he became a leading Black newspaper editor and head of the influential Brotherhood of Sleeping Car Porters labor union. During World War II it was Randolph who urged President Franklin D. Roosevelt to sign orders prohibiting racial segregation in all war industries, and in 1948 he helped to convince President Harry S. Truman to desegregate the U.S. armed forces. In his later years, Randolph organized numerous marches on Washington, including the 1963 Poor People's March, at which Martin Luther King, Jr., gave his famous "I Have a Dream" speech. King himself was of Irish descent on his paternal grandmother's side and had some American Indian ancestry as well.

Several interrelated factors explain the "light at the top" phenomenon in Black American leadership. In a society that is politically and economically controlled by Whites, those members of minorities with the lightest skin and the most Caucasian-looking features have been allowed the greatest freedom. The unique privileges granted to mulattoes under slavery enabled them to advance further, educationally and occupationally, than Blacks who were dark skinned. The result was a leadership pool of light-skinned Blacks with both money and education. Within that pool, it was often those Blacks light enough to pass who became the Black community's most vocal and active leaders.

There is also the peculiar one-drop rule to take into account in any explanation of why so many Black leaders have been light skinned and of mixed ancestry. In *Who Is Black?*, the sociologist F. James Davis analyzes the curious way in which America racially categorizes its citizens. In most other nations around the world, looking White makes one White, but in the United States, a person who has just "one drop" of Black blood is considered Black. When light-skinned Black leaders like Walter White traveled abroad, they had to contend with puzzled Europeans who kept insisting that they were not Black. The expectation that racially mixed Americans will identify with their minority race definitively shapes these individuals' social and political experiences. (If the United States had applied the one-drop rule as rigidly to anyone possessing Native American ancestry, would we also have a history of White-looking Native Americans fighting for their civil and economic rights?)

During the political upheavals of the 1960s, the importance of skin color seemed to diminish. Light-skinned to medium-toned Blacks like Andrew Young, Jesse Jackson, Adam Clayton Powell III, Julian Bond, Kathleen Cleaver, and Angela Davis joined forces with brown-toned to black-toned leaders like Bobby Seale, Eldridge Cleaver, H. Rap Brown, Stokely Carmichael, and Huey Newton to create a new social order. Yet while the Black community appeared united on the surface, undercurrents of colorism still rippled below. Writer Bonnie Allen, in an article in *Essence,* has described what happened to her during one sixties protest.

My most vivid memory of that time period is of being on the courthouse steps in Oakland, Calif. Two thousand demonstrators were screaming, "Free Huey, or the sky's the limit." There I was in the crowd, just being Black, when two Panthers came up to me and said, "Things are going to get rough, so you'd better go home. You're too pretty to get your face messed up." I guess it didn't matter if the rest of the women who remained at the demonstration—some darker than I and more befitting the physical image of a revolutionary Black woman—had their faces messed up. Apparently it wouldn't be a tremendous loss to the Black community. So much for "Black is Beautiful."

In proclaiming "Black is Beautiful," some dark-skinned leaders even questioned the militancy of light-skinned Black radicals, believing that they had benefited too long from color privilege to understand oppression. Dedication to the Black cause was occasionally judged by how well someone's nonkinky hair could be styled in an Afro, or by how willing a light-skinned radical was to sleep with someone who was darker.

Meanwhile, among less radical Blacks, old patterns of color prejudice remained. In an unusual research project conducted in 1968, anthropologist Melville Herkovits measured the lightness of skin and width of facial features in Blacks of two different socioeconomic groups living in Harlem. The well-to-do men were found to have generally lighter skin color, and their noses were an average of 3.8 millimeters narrower than those of men in the poorer segment of the research group. Similarly, the average lip thickness in the well-to-do group was 1 millimeter less than the thickness found in the other group (19.8 millimeters versus 20.8). Because of the highly sensitive nature of this research—and perhaps because measuring lips and noses seems demeaning—no one has dared to repeat it, but presumably the trend holds.

Nearly three decades after the Black Power movement, African Americans can claim some impressive political victories. Consider the following elected or appointed Black leaders: Robert Weaver, secretary of the Department of Housing and Urban Development, the first Black U.S. cabinet member (1966); Edward W. Brooke, the first Black senator since Reconstruction (1966); Thurgood Marshall, the first Black Supreme Court justice (1967); Maynard Jackson, the first Black mayor of Atlanta (1974); Andrew Young, the first Black U.S. ambassador to the United Nations (1976); Patricia R. Harris, the first

Black woman cabinet member (1976); Ernest Morial—or "Dutch," as he liked to be called—the first Black mayor of New Orleans (1977); David Dinkins, the first Black mayor of New York (1989); Douglas Wilder of Virginia, the first Black governor (1989); General Colin L. Powell, the first Black chairman of the Joint Chiefs of Staff (1989); Ron Brown, the first Black to chair the Democratic National Committee (1989); Sharon Pratt (Dixon) Kelly, the first Black female mayor of a major city, Washington, D.C. (1990). Each has achieved considerable success in a country whose political structure is dominated by Whites. Look closely at the faces of these "first" Black leaders, however, and notice what they have in common: they all have light skin. Black Power is far from being literally the case.

What was true in the past holds true today, and not every contemporary Black leader is on the lighter side of the color barometer. A few, including Shirley Chisholm, the first Black congresswoman (1968), Barbara Jordan, a congresswoman from Texas (1972), Harold Washington, the first Black mayor of Chicago (1983), Maxine Waters, a congresswoman from California (1990), and Supreme Court Justice Clarence Thomas (1991), are relatively dark. Nonetheless, the perception lingers that skin color determines how wide the doors of opportunity will open for African Americans. Those who are light skinned have a better chance at succeeding in politics and business, achieving a higher education, and gaining social status than do those who are dark.

For light-skinned Blacks, it simply remains easier to get ahead. Take a close look at Black urban professionals, or "buppies," with their corporate salaries, middle-class values, and predominantly light-brown to medium-brown skin color. They benefit not only from their social contacts with other light-skinned Blacks but also from looks that, in a predominantly White society, are more mainstream. Research conducted by sociologists Veran M. Keith and Cedric Herring in 1991 confirms that skin color remains one of the "present-day mechanisms that influence who gets what in America." Keith and Herring found that, compared to light-skinned Blacks, those with dark skin had less income and a lower standing in the Black community.

In 1990, sociologists Michael Hughes and Bradley Hertel examined whether skin color per se had any influence on the earning potential of Black Americans. Black male and female interviewers surveyed a representative sample of Blacks about their education, income, and social relationships and unobtrusively rated the participants on skin color. After the elimination of differences stemming from socioeconomic background, such as the possibility that light-skinned Blacks came from more prosperous families, the data still reflected the influence of skin color: the light-skinned Blacks fared better educationally and occupationally than their darker peers. To their astonishment, Hughes and Hertel also discovered that the ratio of difference in earnings between the light-skinned and the dark-skinned Blacks was proportional to that between Whites and Blacks. For every 72 cents a dark-skinned Black made, a light-skinned Black earned a dollar. Even today, it appears that blacks with the lightest skin color have the best chances for success.

By contrast, those with the darkest skin color have the hardest time getting ahead. Drive past any inner-city housing project, and you cannot help but notice that the majority of residents are dark skinned. Even more disturbing, look behind the walls of the nation's prisons; they are filled with a disproportionate number of dark-skinned inmates. (A telling saying in the Black community is "The lighter the skin, the lighter the sentence.") While it is possible to trace the color-and-crime connection to differing opportunities for education and success, the suspicion that dark-skinned Blacks, especially men, are more criminally dangerous lurks in the American psyche. When George Bush ran for the presidency in 1988, his infamous television ad featured Willie Horton, a bearded, darker-skinned Black man from Massachusetts who while on a prison furlough committed more crime. This commercial effectively preyed on Whites' fears that the Democratic candidate, Massachusetts Governor Michael Dukakis, would be soft on issues of law and order.

Survey research conducted by sociologist Ozzie Edwards indicates that dark-skinned Blacks are significantly more likely to report being victims of race discrimination than are those of a lighter complexion. And if they are dark-skinned and lower class, they may suffer even more. In comparison, those who are dark but middle class can overcome the negative color stereotype if they adopt mainstream values and have the resources to dress well and pursue a higher education. And Blacks who are lower class but light skinned are more readily trusted by the general public, particularly by White employers. As a result, impoverished light-skinned youths may find it easier to get jobs and break free of the cycle of poverty and crime that plagues their darker-skinned counterparts.

Within the Black community, skin color is not often a factor in the political campaigns of Black candidates because they usually are running against White or Latino opponents, and Blacks of different backgrounds tend to come together to support one of their own. However, when two or more Black politicians with different skin tones (and backgrounds) face off against each other in an election, color bias may indeed enter the race. Some Black voters distrust very light skinned Blacks, perceiving them as elitist and out of touch. Given a choice, these voters prefer medium-skinned to dark-skinned candidates, believing that they identify more closely with issues affecting the Black community. When the fair-skinned, fine-featured Sharon Pratt (Dixon) Kelly ran for mayor of the District of Columbia, following Marion Barry's embarrassing encounter with the law, her complexion became an issue. Many of the city's poorest residents, living in the most crime-infested neighborhoods, seriously questioned whether Dixon could understand their problems. Despite his legal difficulties, some remained loyal to the darker-skinned Barry.

The impact of skin color on the realization of the American dream seems obvious, yet many African Americans continue to deny its importance. A black woman serving as the academic vice president of a large midwestern university dismisses the possibility that in this post-sixties era a gap in power and income could be based on something as superficial as skin color. She admits, however, that Black men still prefer lighter-skinned women. Another professional, a highly successful insurance lawyer from New Jersey, reacted with genuine surprise when he learned of the significant difference in earning potential between light-skinned and dark-skinned Blacks. Both the law-yer and the university official have skin color in the light-brown to mid-brown range. For them and others like them, color tone has not seemed a very important factor in their lives. It is primarily those who are either very dark or very light who are affected the most by the color gap in power and privilege.

3. Embracing Whiteness

Wouldn't they be surprised when one day I woke out of my black ugly dream,
and my real hair, which was long and blond, would take the place of the kinky
mass that Momma wouldn't let me straighten? . . . Because I was really white
and because a cruel fairy stepmother, who was understandably jealous of my
beauty, had turned me into a too-big Negro girl, with nappy black hair, broad
feet and a space between her teeth that would hold a number-two pencil.
—MAYA ANGELOU,

I Know Why the Caged Bird Sings

Countless Black girls in the United States share the fantasy of being White. How could it be otherwise in a society whose ideal beauty— blond, pale skinned, with blue or green eyes—embodies everything the average Black female lacks?

In fact, the desire for lighter skin is nearly universal. Throughout Central and South America, Asia, and even Africa, society is prejudiced against those with dark skin, especially young dark women. Various theories for this have been advanced, but in a race-stratified society like America the consequences have long been clear. Before the Civil War, the degree of pigmentation could mean the difference between living free and enslavement, and since then variations in skin color and features have divided the educated from the ignorant, the well-off from the poor, the "attractive" from the "plain."

Throughout this disturbing history Black women have demanded secret formulas and special techniques to keep them from looking "too Negroid." Our society values beauty in women to the same degree that it values intelligence, political influence, and physical strength in men. While thousands of Black men have felt the effects of their dark coloring and broad features, dark-skinned females have suffered far more. A dark-skinned Black man can use his intelligence to compensate for his "unfortunate coloring," and if he is financially secure he may marry a light-skinned woman, thereby improving his own social position and that of his children. A dark-skinned Black woman who feels herself unattractive, however, may think that she has nothing to offer society no matter how intelligent or inventive she is.

The pain of being a dark-skinned female is a common theme in Black literature. In Wallace Thurman's 1929 book, *The Blacker the Berry*, the blue-black Emma Lou reflects on her skin color.

> She should have been a boy, then color of skin wouldn't have mattered so much, for wasn't her mother always saying that a black boy could get along, but that a black girl would never know anything but sorrow and disappointment? But she wasn't a boy; she was a girl, and color did matter, mattered so much that she would rather have missed receiving her high school diploma than have to sit as she now sat, the only odd and conspicuous figure on the auditorium platform of the Boise high school.

In Toni Morrison's *The Bluest Eye*, the dark-skinned Claudia reacts with murderous rage when she gets an Aryan-looking doll for Christmas.

> I destroy white baby dolls. . . . But the dismembering of dolls was not the true horror. The true horrifying thing was the transference of the same impulses to little white girls. The indifference with which I could have axed them was shaken only by my desire to do so. To discover what eluded me: the secret of the magic they weaved on others. What made people look at them and say, "Awwwww," but not for me? The eye slide of black women as they approached them on the street, and the possessive gentleness of their touch as they handled them.

And in Maya Angelou's semiautobiographical *I Know Why the Caged Bird Sings*, the protagonist muses about how much better her life would be if she could just wake up from her "black ugly dream." In each of these works the message is clear: darkness causes suffering; lightness brings love.

According to psychiatrists William Grier and Price Cobbs, authors of *Black Rage*, every American Black girl experiences some degree of shame about her appearance. Many must submit to painful hair-combing rituals that aim to make them look, if not more "Whitelike," at least more "presentable." As they grow older they begin to use special products designed to straighten and manage kinky, unruly hair and to bleach dark skin.

Fortunately, or perhaps unfortunately, there is no shortage of products especially designed for the Black woman. The cosmetics and beauty businesses are among the most profitable within the Black community. Entrepreneurs like George Johnson, the founder and chief executive of Johnson Products Company (which makes Ultra Sheen and Ultra Wave), are occasionally accused of getting rich off Black women's insecurities. Johnson has given a candid response to such criticism:

> What's wrong with that? The need was always there. With my products, I set about fulfilling it. Many black women wish their skins were lighter, [or] their hair were straighter. Our makeup lightens their skins, our relaxers straighten their hair and make these women happier with themselves.

These beauty practices have a long history. While still under the cruel and dehumanizing conditions of slavery, many Negro women tried to alter the texture and appearance of their hair. Most of the time, a slave woman kept her head wrapped in a "do-rag," or bandanna, but on special occasions she might straighten her hair with some kind of grease, as her African ancestors may have done. House servants fared better in this regard because they had access to hog lard, margarine, or butter. Sometimes they could even borrow "Miss Ann's" fine scissors to give themselves a stylish trim. But field hands had to use shears and axle grease, which was not only tough to remove but also caused the hair to stretch and break.

Following the Civil War, fashionable mulattoes valued hair that was straight, and in attempting to emulate them, other Negro women aimed for a processed look. Some used a "mammy-leg" cap—the leg of a woman's stocking pulled over greased hair. When it was removed, hours later, the hair was flatter, but the cap worked only so well, and humid weather quickly made the hair go back to its natural state. The demand grew for more effective methods of hair straightening.

With her invention of a special scalp and hair-preparation formula, Sarah Breedlove, better known as Madam (a common title of respect used by Black businesswomen) C. J. Walker, was among the first to tap the hair-straightening market. From *Madam C. J Walker: Entrepreneur,* a biography written by her great-great-granddaughter A'Lelia P. Bundles, much is known about her life. Born of former slaves in the Louisiana delta in 1867, four years after emancipation, Sarah was orphaned at five and married at fourteen. By the time she reached her twenties she was a widowed single parent. Soon after that her hair started falling out. She claimed that when things were at their worst, she had a vision in which an old man revealed the secret ingredients of a formula that would make her scalp and hair healthy. She hunted down the recommended ingredients, primarily a mixture of petrolatum and sulphur. Madam Walker also maintained—perhaps a reflection on her business savvy—that the mixture contained secret ingredients grown in Africa. At the turn of the century, the best-selling patent medicines and other products tended to credit some miracle or mystery for their effectiveness. To her delight, she discovered the secret formula actually worked and quickly realized that other Black women could benefit from her secret. Before long the "Walker System of Beauty Culture" had become so popular that she found it necessary to move her operations to a larger city.

In 1910, by the age of forty-three, Madam Walker was operating an impressive factory and laboratory in Indianapolis, where she not only mass-produced her secret formula but also trained others in the Walker hair care technique. Beauticians were taught how to wash and oil the scalp and then press the hair, using a European hot comb that Walker had redesigned for Black women. The Walker hot comb could be heated either on a special burner that her agents sold separately, or on a regular stove. However, if the comb got too hot, the hair could easily burn.

In addition to her hair formula and hot comb, Walker sold various toiletries and cosmetics, including face powders, bath oils, lotions, soaps, and health aids. She marketed her merchandise so aggressively throughout the United States and Europe that in 1910 the *Guinness Book of World Records* identified Madam Walker as the first self-made millionairess in history.

Many have called Madam Walker "the hair-straightening queen," but she always denied that her products were hair straighteners and forbade her army of saleswomen to use the word "straightener" when discussing her merchandise. She particularly resented accusations that her products were intended to make Black women look White. Walker always claimed that her primary concern was the Black woman who suffered from dry scalp and hair breakage. Her products were intended to beautify the Black woman, she said, and in the process give her more, not less, confidence. In 1917, she stated, "Right here let me correct the erroneous impression held by some that I claim to straighten the hair. I want the great masses of my people to take a greater pride in their personal appearance and to give their hair proper attention." And it was certainly no secret that many, if not most, Black women were dissatisfied with or ashamed of their hair. As a verse from a turn-of-the-century song entitled "Nappy Headed Blues" put it:

> *My hair is cantcha, don'tcha.*
> *You can't comb it.*
> *Don'tcha try.*
> *Nappy, that's the reason why.*

Black ministers and leaders were among those who protested the use of hair-straightening products. Disapproving preachers would thunderously proclaim, "If God wanted you to have straight hair, He would have given it to you." Yet as A'Lelia Bundles wryly notes,

"I wonder how many of these same men were also attracted to women with long hair and mulatto looks?"

Although Madam Walker is considered the inventor of the first hair-straightening system for Blacks, this is not entirely true. In the mid-1800s a woman known as Madam Annie M. Turnbo Malone had developed "pullers," which flattened hair by pulling it. But many customers were dissatisfied with the slick, flattened appearance the pullers created and considered Walker's hot comb a vast improvement. (Ironically, an improved version of pullers, called flatirons, has made a comeback in today's Black beauty salons.) Other Black women, too, including Madam Sarah Spencer Washington and Dr. Marjorie Stewart Joyner, who was the national supervisor of all the Walker beauty schools, made their mark and a good deal of money in Black beauty culture.

Although it is easy to criticize, the Black beauty business has helped thousands of Black women achieve financial security. At the turn of the century Walker's products were sold door to door, like today's Mary Kay cosmetics, by saleswomen who earned commissions and competed for various incentives and bonuses. Many Black women, single and married, were able to acquire a degree of financial independence that would otherwise have been unavailable to them. When Madam Walker died in 1919 at the age of fifty-one and at the height of her business success, she stipulated in her will that the president of her company always be a woman. Although the company still operates today, it faces stiff competition from much larger corporations like Johnson Products and SoftSheen.

By the turn of the century the straightening of kinky hair was recognized as big business, and large corporations were catching a ride on the Black beauty bandwagon. Some of the new products were effective, but many others were useless and did nothing more than prey on Black women's fantasies. Slick advertisements for such Black beauty products as permanent hair relaxers and hair dressings were a mainstay of many Negro magazines, including the *Half-Century Magazine, Opportunity, The Messenger,* and *The Crisis.*

The November 1921 issue of the *Half-Century Magazine* contained three ads typical of those for Black hair products: one from the Overton Hygienic Manufacturing Company for a formula called High Brown Hair Grower, promising "A Wealth of Glorious Hair"; another for a product from the Van Tyle Chemical Laboratories called Evergloss, offering that "combed and glossy" look; a third depicting a fine-featured Black woman, with hair longer than that of most White women, touting a product called Mme. C. J. Hart's Hair Grower. Yet another popular Black hair product of the 1920s was Kink No More, which, despite its promising name, required reapplication every two weeks.

Until the 1960s most Black women, and some Black men, regularly straightened their hair. It was rare for a Black woman to be seen in public with unprocessed hair, and those who dared risked the ridicule and even the chastisement of close friends and family members. When the Afro became fashionable during the sixties, it was radical in more ways than one. It not only associated the wearer with the politics of the Black Power movement, but, for women, it also signaled the abandonment of the hair-straightening products they had been conditioned to use since childhood. The Afro eventually went the way of all trendy hairstyles, and by the mid-seventies most Blacks (although not as many as before) had returned to processing their hair.

Today's popular Black magazines, including *Ebony* and *Essence,* still carry prominent ads promising to fix the "Black hair problem." When sociologist Bertice Berry analyzed the advertisements in *Ebony, Jet,* and *Essence* between 1985 and 1987, she found that over a third were for various kinds of hair products. The vast majority of the ads, whether for hair-remedy formulas like Power Gro or for hair weaves, braids, or wigs, used fair-skinned Black models with long, flowing tresses.

One Black model and businesswoman, Naomi Sims, maintains that the use of hair straighteners and dyes should not be considered just a White assimilationist practice. Long before Parisian women of the 1920s made straight hair fashionable, the women of the Swahili and the Hova of Madagascar were straightening their hair with heavy oil and parting it down the center. And "Beatle bangs," named for the hairstyles of the Beatles of the sixties, can be traced back to the women of Chad, who twisted their hair into tiny dreadlocks and then cropped it straight across the forehead. The same is true for hair coloring. Black women who dye their hair a lighter shade are often accused of trying to look White, but for a long time African women have been coloring their hair with henna, ocher, plant dyes, and other natural substances. In one tribe, women traditionally dye their hair blond, a cosmetic practice hardly related to wanting to be White.

Some African Americans also cosmetically alter their eye color. Ever since the invention of the tinted contact lens, there have been Whites as well as Blacks, men as well as women—including some with twenty-twenty vision—who have opted to lighten their eye color. The earliest tinted lenses tended to look artificial; now an improved version blends two different shades for a more natural appearance. As a result, the popularity of tinted lenses is on the rise again, especially among Black women.

Most print and TV ads for tinted contact lenses make no mention of correcting the wearer's vision but instead promise to "improve" eye color. The message—that brown eyes are unacceptable and blue eyes are better—blankets predominantly Black urban neighborhoods on billboards and in Black magazines. Elsie B. Washington, a senior editor of *Essence,* is disturbed by the phenomenon.

> . . . the wish to acquire what we were not born with, to adopt the coloring that has for centuries been touted as prettier, finer, better, carries with it all the old baggage of racial inferiority and/or superiority based simply, and simplistically, on physical traits. White America, its institutions, its industrial machine, has always been very clear on the looks that it prizes: in five words, blond hair and blue eyes.

Not every Black woman with green or blue eyes is necessarily wearing contact lenses, though. Many Black women are born with eye color other than brown. Even so, when the April 1982 cover of *Essence* featured a naturally blue-eyed Black model, the editors were swamped with hundreds of letters from angry readers who interpreted the magazine's choice of cover girl as a denial of Black beauty. Clearly,

Black women who do not happen to possess the politically correct eye color should not be suspect, but, then, perhaps neither should every brown-eyed Black woman who chooses to wear green or blue contact lenses.

Not only are hair texture and eye color loaded symbols for many African Americans, so is the shape of the nose. For a few thousand dollars, an undesirable nose can be surgically reshaped into a narrow proboscis with just the right upward tilt—something more than a few Jewish women are known to have had done. Yet most people who seek nasal surgery do not desire Caucasian features, according to W. Earle Matory, Jr., M.D., Associate Professor of Plastic Surgery at the University of Massachusetts Medical Center in Worcester. Dr. Matory, who has spent the last ten years studying how perceptions of a beautiful face differ between members of various ethnic groups, claims that in performing cosmetic surgery on people of color, his goal is to preserve the ethnic character of the face while improving the aesthetic appearance of one or more features. For example, an African-American woman may seek elevation of a flat nasal bridge, or a man may decide to have his nose narrowed because it is unusually wide for his ethnic group. However, if a patient specifically requests the physical features characteristic of another ethnic group, Dr. Matory recommends that the individual seek psychological counseling instead.

Surgery is expensive, though, and among women, many choose instead a makeup technique that de-emphasizes a broad nose: the application of darker shades of liquid base along the bottom and sides of the nose, lighter tones along the top—a method that looks painfully obvious if overdone. Another, more desperate measure is to sleep with a clothespin clipped over the nose—something that Oprah Winfrey confesses to having tried when she was young. Probably the only thing affected was a good night's rest.

Hair texture, eye color, and nose shape are all features that African Americans can modify if they want to and are able to pay. The color of skin, the most visible feature of the body, is more difficult to change. But that doesn't mean that many haven't tried.

American Negro women of the nineteenth century sometimes

rubbed lye directly on their skin, and others applied harsh acidic products made for removing dirt and grime from floors and walls. There were also homemade concoctions of lemon juice, bleach, or urine to smear on the skin and arsenic wafers to swallow, all designed to "get the dark out." None of these methods worked, and all of them smelled, burned, or worse. One nineteenth-century mother tried unsuccessfully to lighten her unacceptably dark daughter by dunking her every day in a tub of bleach.

After hair straighteners hit the market, entrepreneurs were quick to realize that skin-bleaching products could also be wildly profitable. Packaged in attractive boxes and given fancy names, most of this early merchandise contained nothing more than chalk and grease. Later, formulas were developed that actually did lighten the color of the skin, but these were so harsh that they usually left the skin blotchy, dry, and damaged.

One skin-bleaching product that was particularly popular during the twenties was Ro-Zol bleach. Distributed by the Black-owned Overton Hygienic Manufacturing Company, Ro-Zol was originally developed as a solution to remove various skin defects and discolorations, but it was subsequently marketed more profitably as a whitening agent. In one Ro-Zol ad, a fabulously wealthy-looking Black couple is shown at a table covered with a starched white linen cloth, sipping tea from fine china cups. The woman, who is several shades lighter than the man, is admiring herself in a small mirror, obviously pleased with the results of Ro-Zol. The ad reads:

> Ro-Zol was the first preparation made expressly for bleaching. . . . Ro-Zol does not bleach by destroying the pigmentation. . . . It is received by the pigment and combines and harmonizes to produce a remarkably satisfactory, youthful, wholesome and *whitened* complexion.

A more blatant advertisement for a bleaching cream solicited customers with this copy: "Lighten your dark skin. Race men and women, protect your future by using Black & White Ointment. Be attractive. Throw off the chains that have held you back from the prosperity that rightly belongs to you.'' Such ads were clearly designed to tap both Black men's and Black women's insecurities about being dark. And apparently they worked—products like Ro-Zol made a fortune.

Perhaps the most outlandish claim came from a biologist, Dr. Yusaburo Noguchi, a respected member of the Japanese Academy of Medicine. Dr. Noguchi stated, in the November 1929 issue of *The Literary Digest,* that a time was coming when ''parents of children with colored skin can have the pigment changed so that the Negro or the papoose will have the white skin of a Scandinavian.'' Although he declined to elaborate further on the results of his fifteen years of scientific research, Dr. Noguchi hinted that through electrical nutrition and glandular control an ''infant body might change potentialities'' and that ''small people [could] be made large and colored skins be bleached of their darkness, be it black, brown, red or yellow.'' (Inspired by Dr. Noguchi's fantastic claims, the satirist George Schuyler wrote a best-selling novel, *Black No More,* about a scientist who invented a machine that could magically transform Black people into Whites.)

Today, skin-bleaching products such as Nadinola (which dates back to 1889), Ambi Fade Creme, Esoterica, Porcelana, and Vantex continue to be plucked off the shelves by thousands of African-American women. In 1990 alone, some $44 million worth of skin-bleaching products were purchased. According to one regular user, the majority of Black women who buy these products are not trying to look White. ''Most Black women just want to bleach out their freckles and smooth out any patches of discoloration,'' this woman claims. Then she added, ''They have to keep using the fade cream because if they stop, the freckles and discoloration just come right back.''

The active ingredient in most over-the-counter skin-bleaching creams is hydroquinone, a chemical whose melanin-inhibiting properties were discovered quite by accident. In June of 1938, workers in the Greiss-Pflieger tannery in Waukegan, Illinois, were issued new rubber gloves that contained monobenzyl ether of hydroquinone (HQ), a substance designed both to reinforce the gloves and to prevent discoloration of the leather the workers handled. Black employees in the plant soon began to complain about the appearance of bleached spots on their arms and hands—although apparently a few were complimented on their lighter-looking hands and arms. The hydroquinone-washed gloves were recalled, but not before eighteen Black men at the plant had filed suit against the company and won settlements ranging from $75 to $900.

The tannery experience awakened entrepreneurs to hydroquinone's skin-bleaching qualities. In tests of the chemical's safety and effectiveness, researchers found that, while hydroquinone in small doses can safely lighten the skin of most people, a small percentage is intensely allergic to it. A representative of the American Academy of Dermatology in Chicago described the case of one Black woman hypersensitive to HQ whose skin turned navy blue. More recent investigations into the safety of HQ suggest that, in rats and mice, the substance may cause cancer, and in humans it sometimes causes a paradoxical darkening of skin called exogenous ochrinosis.

Because of new findings about the safety of HQ, South Africa moved in 1990 to ban all over-the-counter sales of skin bleaches. There are a growing number of health officials in this country, including Mark Green, Commissioner of New York's Department of Consumer Affairs, who are asking the Food and Drug Administration to do the same. At the very least, these products should be better labeled. Few of them warn consumers that following application of products containing HQ, the skin may darken under direct sunlight unless a Sunscreen Protection Factor (SPF) of at least 20 is used. Despite such risks, dermatologists report that some Black patients still request prescriptions of HQ stronger than the 2 percent concentration available in over-the-counter preparations.

Blacks seeking lighter skin can also go to special salons where, for a price, full or partial body bleaches are available. Sudie Hidary, a skin-care specialist who has worked at both the prestigious Georgette Klinger and F8th salons in Beverly Hills, says that the salons' mostly female patrons usually have only the face and neck bleached. Full bleaching is expensive and requires a shower afterward, to avoid burning, and protection from direct sunlight. In fact, Hidary believes that skin bleaching may explain why the increasingly lighter-looking Michael Jackson has been seen in public wearing a large bag over his head. LaToya Jackson claims, however, that in 1979 her brother Michael was diagnosed with lupus, a rare disorder that causes skin lesions and necessitates staying out of the sun.

For those willing to go to drastic lengths to "brighten" a "dull" complexion, there are two surgical procedures, chemical peels and dermabrasion. Chemical peels, which are extremely painful and require hospitalization, involve the burning off of the top layer of pigmentation to uncover the smoother, lighter layer underneath. Several follow-up visits are needed, and the entire process can take as long as a year before the skin is lightened effectively. The price of a chemical peel, according to the American Society of Plastic and Reconstructive Surgeons, ranges from $1,640 to $3,000.

Dermabrasion, which is still more painful, involves stripping away the uppermost layers of skin with high-speed wire or diamond-edged brushes. Dr. Robert Auerbach, a dermatologist affiliated with New York University, likens it to "skinning your knee on the sidewalk." His colleague, Thomas Rees, warns that both abrasion and peeling traumatize the skin: "With either procedure, the skin can be removed too deeply and result in an open wound, and deaths from cardiac arrest have followed." Dermabrasion costs anywhere from $1,260 to $3,000.

Black women with no desire to bleach their skin sometimes prefer to use liquid facial makeup several shades lighter than their actual color. But Black businesswoman Barbara Walden, the founder of Barbara Walden Cosmetics, is trying to change the "looking lighter is better" attitude with products designed to match the many shades of African-American women's skin. Walden points out that Black women, particularly older ones, sometimes avoid makeup that matches their skin tones. When such a woman complains, "Don't put that on me because I don't want to be that dark. I want to be lighter," Walden admonishes her: "This is your complexion and we are going to work with your skin tone. If you want to be lighter, you'll have to go somewhere else and use other products." Walden says that most

White-owned cosmetic companies have not bothered to formulate skin products for African-American women, and as a result many have resigned themselves to wearing cosmetics intended for White women's skin. Although "White" liquid makeup can give a Black woman a somewhat lighter appearance, it usually leaves her with an ashy-looking residue that ends abruptly at the neck. Still, many Black women think they look better in makeup that is substantially lighter than their actual color.

The desire to lighten one's skin and alter one's features can be seen as a form of Black self-hatred. Yet Black women who straighten their hair or bleach their skin are in a sense behaving no differently than women of other cultures, who bind their feet or tighten corsets around their waists to achieve a culturally defined feminine appearance. Still, the reactions of Blacks to the grooming habits of other Blacks are deeply rooted and complex. When a White woman with brown eyes wears blue contact lenses, she might be thought vain for doing so, but most people would not assume that she was denying her heritage. When a White woman bakes under the hot sun all day to tan her pale skin, she might be admonished for risking skin cancer, but few would conclude that she hates being White. And when a White woman perms her straight hair, she is rarely accused of wanting to be something that she is not. But nearly everything the Black woman (or man) does to her (or his) appearance is interpreted politically.

Throughout American history degrees of skin coloring and kinkiness of hair have had the power to shape the quality of Black people's lives. Thus it is no surprise that a heightened sensitivity has developed around issues of appearance. On the surface, Whites and Blacks might each seem to imitate the other's looks, but the political dimensions of their actions—based on the gap in power between the two groups—are very different. When a thin-lipped White actress gets a collagen injection to give her a more sensual Negroid-looking mouth, or when a White rock musician wears dreadlocks for a more "streetwise" appearance, it is simply not the same as when a Black woman straightens her hair or goes to great lengths to avoid prolonged sunlight. Whites can dabble in practices that make them appear more

Black, but for many African Americans embracing Whiteness is a matter of economic, social, or political survival.*

Social scientists have advanced various theories to explain the widespread preference for lighter skin and straighter hair. The first theory contends that the "establishment" sets standards for behavior and appearance and that those who strive for success must conform accordingly. Standards change only after enough members of a subordinate group have moved into positions of power. In the seventies, for example, when women began to enter white-collar occupations that had previously been reserved for men, they typically wore tailored suits with shoulder pads, oxford-cloth shirts, and bow ties—an imitation of the male uniform. Since then, the presence of a greater number of females in corporate positions has made dresses and other tokens of femininity more acceptable. Similarly, as Blacks move into positions of power a growing number are daring to look less "European." This is particularly true in professions that value freedom of expression: Black professors and journalists, both male and female, now routinely sport African garb and unprocessed hair.

A related theory holds that the "White is right" attitude accompanied the European conquest of the globe. When the Portuguese invaded Brazil in the sixteenth century, for example, they established a color hierarchy remarkably similar to our own. The lighter-skinned Portuguese subdued the brown-skinned Indian natives and the Africans who were imported as slaves. To this day, while the vast majority of Brazilians (80 percent) are of African or Indian descent, Brazil remains a country predominantly controlled by Whites. Nearly half of all Afro-Brazilians live in contaminated housing and work in menial jobs paying less than $50 per month, and relatively few are wealthy or influential in politics. Power and coloring are so closely

---

*Although Blacks occasionally accuse Whites who seek a tan of subconsciously trying to become Black, they are more likely seeking to communicate social status. While pale skin once meant one had been spared from outdoor labor, after the industrial revolution, when much of the working class left the farm for factories, a tan came to represent membership in a class that had plenty of leisure time. In the jet age, a wintertime tan signals sophistication and freedom to travel. Because tanning is associated with class more than with femininity, it is the one vanity indulged in by as many White men as White women. The obsession with tanning seems to have peaked, though, and pallor is again gaining status, as a symbol of education and health consciousness.

linked in Brazil that when the soccer player Pele became an international celebrity, he was able to declare himself no longer Black.

Similarly, throughout much of South and Central America people with brown or black skin tones are at a disadvantage. Many Latin-American countries, including Mexico, have relatively small middle classes, so issues of class and color become exaggerated: either a person is light skinned and privileged or dark skinned and poor.

Even in parts of Africa, one can find a preference for light skin coloring. Alice Windom, coordinator of the James T. Bush, Sr., Center at the University of Missouri-St. Louis, believes that the arrival of Whites in Africa contaminated the indigenous culture. While in Africa in the sixties, Windom observed a number of dark-skinned African women, mostly in countries formerly under British rule, using bleaching creams and special soaps so that they, too, could look "English." Some urban Zambian women began applying bleaching products so strong that government officials criticized them for having "Fanta faces and Coca-Cola bodies," Fanta being a popular orange-colored carbonated beverage. Recently, Nigerian government officials even implored British manufacturers to stop exporting bleaching products to their country because some of their citizens were experiencing skin damage.

A variation of the conquest hypothesis is Dr. Frances Cress Welsing's theory of color confrontation. Pointing to two indisputable facts, that Whites are color deficient and that color-deficient people represent a minority of the world's population, Welsing asks why White people have tried so hard to conquer non-White, melanin-producing populations. She offers a psychoanalytic answer: when Whites realized that color was the norm and that its absence was abnormal, deep-seated feelings of inferiority and inadequacy drove them to conquer those who possessed the attribute they lacked. Welsing cites three primary defense mechanisms to explain this behavior: (1) repression, the tendency to deny pain, in this case the pain of being a colorless minority; (2) reaction formation, the tendency to relegate that which is desirable (color) to that which is disdained; and (3) projection, the tendency to blame others (people of color) for the hatred one feels.

Intraracial color discrimination may similarly be viewed from a psychoanalytic perspective. In a defensive reaction known as "identification with the aggressor," the oppressed imitate the oppressors in order to survive. This phenomenon (the same one that leads abused children vigorously to defend their abusive parents) could explain why, in a racist society, light-skinned Blacks identify with Whites, but discriminate against Blacks who are darker.

Psycho-sociological theories like these might adequately explain color prejudice were it not for one important fact: around the world, ancient stories and proverbs praising the value of pale skin, especially in women, long preceded the arrival of the White man. In Central America, thousands of years ago, bronze-brown Aztec women during courtship used to smear themselves with an ointment made of yellow earth, since golden skin was considered more attractive than brown.

Hundreds of years before any contact with Westerners, the Japanese treasured white skin in women. An ancient proverb had it that "White skin makes up for seven defects." *The Tale of Genji,* Lady Murasaki's famous eleventh-century chronicle, contains several references to the desirability of white-skinned women, and in feudal Japan, noblewomen painted their faces white. Even today, white skin is considered essential to feminine beauty, and many Japanese women carry parasols to protect their skin from the sun.

In India, where attitudes about skin color are complicated by the highly stratified caste system, northern Indians discriminate against southern Indians simply because the latter are darker. There, too, the preference for light skin, especially in women, seems to have existed long before any contact with European cultures. In many ancient Indian languages (as well as in Shakespeare's English), the words "fair" and "beautiful" are interchangeable, and the most desirable brides are often described as those whose "skin is as pale as the moon."

In Arab countries, the highest admiration is reserved for the woman who is as white as snow—strange praise indeed in lands where snow hardly ever falls. Yet an ancient Moroccan proverb warns young men against the superficial attractions of the pale-skinned wife: "A fertile negress is better than a sterile white woman." Throughout the Muslim world, the upper class is light skinned and the lower class is darker.

Even among Whites, especially females, a peaches-and-cream complexion is considered a sign of aristocratic refinement. In her book *Femininity,* Susan Brownmiller examines art history for evidence of a sex-linked preference for light skin. She finds that ancient Egyptian artists dipped into lighter hues, like yellow, when painting the female body and reserved the darker, more reddish colors for males. And in classical Western art, the ideal woman is nearly always shell pink, while men are painted in earthier tones. Light skin is considered not only more beautiful, but also more feminine.

The Human Relations Area Files, an anthropological listing of 312 different cultures, reveals that in 51 cultures skin color is a criterion of beauty, and that in all but 4 of these, lighter skin is preferred. A notable exception is the Toba culture of Bolivia, whose menstruating women used to attract men by painting their faces black. Since ovulation occurs two weeks prior to menstruation, one has to wonder exactly how reproductively selective this practice was.

Some contemporary anthropologists believe that the desire for light skin in females has a sex-linked biological basis. Charles Darwin even thought that was the case. As early as 1874, he surmised, in *The Descent of Man,* that sexual selection favored light skin in women but not in men. Two recent evolutionary theories attempt to explain why this might be so.

The first, known as the neotenous hypothesis, is based on the idea that light skin signals youthfulness. Childlike characteristics in women apparently call forth a nurturing instinct in men, leading to stronger pair bonding and better protection of offspring. A growing body of research indicates that men are attracted not only to a "baby face," but also to other childish traits in adult women: a high proportion of body fat (the female obsession with thinness is uniquely Western), a high-pitched voice, large eyes, and a small nose.

The second hypothesis links skin color more directly with femininity and fertility. An old Hopi saying supports this view: "A woman with a dark skin may be half man." Scientists have observed that although human skin tends to darken in both sexes from birth onward, starting at puberty the skin of females tends to darken less rapidly. Even in studies that have screened out such environmental factors as men's more prolonged exposure to the sun, there seems to be a significant difference between the sexes. The hair of blond males also darkens more quickly after puberty than the hair of blond females. A woman's skin does not usually darken as much as a man's until after a pregnancy. Thus on an instinctual level, men may perceive fair-skinned females as "virgins" still available for reproductive purposes.

In 1965, scientists from around the world gathered in Copenhagen for a conference on race and color, the aim of which was to improve understanding of worldwide discrimination based on skin color. Among the matters they considered was a possible link between prejudice and religious images of good and evil. One proposal posited that the entire conflict between Christ and Satan, spirit and flesh, good and evil, could be summarized as a conflict between White and Black. One of the participants, Roger Bastide, described the deliberate whitening of Christ as revisionists transformed him from a Semite to an Aryan.

> The dark hair that Christ was thought to have had came to be rendered as very light colored, and his big dark eyes as blue. It was necessary that this man, the incarnation of God, be as far removed as possible from everything that could suggest darkness or blackness, even indirectly. His hair and his beard were given the color of sunshine, the brightness of the light above, while his eyes retained the color of the sky from which he descended and to which he returned.

Some scientists concluded that language symbolism is indeed an important source of bias against those who are darker. We talk of "dark deeds," "black sheep," "blackballing," and "blacklisting," and we talk of "good guys dressed in white" and "pure as the driven snow." Even the definitions of the words "black" and "white," excerpted from *Webster's Third New International Dictionary,* give credence to the notion that, by nature, black is bad and white is good.

> **white** free from blemish, moral stain, or impurity; outstandingly righteous; innocent; not marked by malignant influence;

notably pleasing or auspicious; fortunate; notably ardent; decent; in a fair, upright manner; a sterling man; and so on.

black outrageously wicked; a villain; dishonorable; expressing or indicating disgrace, discredit, or guilt; connected with the devil; expressing menace; sullen; hostile; unqualified; connected with a violation of a public regulation; illicit, illegal; affected by some undesirable condition; and so on.

Wallace Thurman was another who recognized the importance of language in shaping attitudes about skin coloring. In *The Blacker the Berry,* an intellectual character named Truman says:

All of you know that white is the symbol of everything pure and good, whether that everything be concrete or abstract. Ivory Soap is advertised as being ninety-nine and some fraction per cent pure, and Ivory Soap is white. Moreover, virtue and virginity are always represented as being clothed in white garments. Then, too, the God we, or rather most Negroes worship is a patriarchal white man, seated on a white throne, in a spotless white Heaven, radiant with white streets and white-apparelled angels eating white honey and drinking white milk.

While these theories about biology and about language symbolism have something to teach us, they cannot address the harsh political consequences of the light-skin preference in a country like South Africa. Until as recently as 1991, when the Population Registration Act was finally revoked, the White minority government required all citizens to be legally classified at birth into one of four distinct categories based on race and coloring: Whites (14.3 percent of the total population in 1991), Colored (8.6 percent), Asian (2.6 percent), and African (74.5 percent). When parents came from two different classes, their children automatically fell into the lower category. It was possible to apply for reclassification—a procedure that entailed standing before a panel of White judges who coolly assessed skin coloring, hair texture, and thickness of lips. There were enormous advantages to being classified Colored rather than African: the Colored class gained the right to vote in 1983, although only for its own parliament, which remained under the domination of the powerful White parliament. Colored persons had greater freedom of movement, larger state pensions, and better housing. A separate school system existed for African children, and, as Winnie Mandela noted, "The lower you are economically and the darker you are, the [worse] your education will be."

As long as differences in skin color determine access to wealth and privilege, many who are dark will continue to search for new and better ways of embracing Whiteness.

4. Black Identity: Shades of Beauty and Pride

Being Black is not a color, it's an experience.
—KATHY RUSSELL

Bertice Berry, a sociologist as well as a stand-up comic, has thought a lot about Black identity. Her doctoral research, completed in 1988, was a serious study of Black-on-Black discrimination. Now, as a comedian, she uses humor to break through the silence that conceals attitudes about color in the Black community. Berry freely jokes about issues of Black beauty, frequently using herself as a point of departure in asking why Black women with dark skin, nappy hair, and big butts are made to feel so bad about themselves. On stage, she describes the day she looked in the mirror and came to the realization that she was never going to look like America's ideal beauty, Black or otherwise. Instead of spending thousands of dollars to change herself, Berry decided that it made better sense to try to change other people's views. Her plan appears to have worked. With her dreadlocks and strong African features, Berry radiates a combination of beauty and racial pride.

Black identity is a multifaceted and in some ways nebulous concept. Being Black affects the way a person walks and talks, his or her values, culture, and history, how that person relates to others and how they relate to him or her. It is governed by one's early social experience, history and politics, conscious input and labeling, and the genetic accident that dictates external appearance. Skin color appears to affect identity, but in complex and seemingly unpredictable ways. Although color has been used as a metaphor for Blackness—never more so than during the sixties—pigmentation alone cannot be used to predict the extent of racial identification. In fact, some of the most Afrocentric people in America are those with the least amount of African ancestry.

Initial awareness of race occurs early in a Black child's life, surfacing sometime between the ages of three and five. Black nursery-school children may understand, for instance, that their hair has a different texture than that of other children in their class. Yet their concept of race will not crystallize for a few more years. Black parents, especially those who have worked hard to instill a strong sense of racial pride in their offspring, often become angry and discouraged when their four- or five-year-old suddenly proclaims, "When I grow up, I'm going to be White," or asks, "When am I going to stop looking so brown?" These parents need not worry, however. Most children younger than five lack the cognitive ability known as concept constancy—in this case, the knowledge that their race will not change over time. The absence of a sense of gender constancy similarly leads little boys to say "When I grow up I'm going to be a mommy." Black parents need not be alarmed to hear their small children speculate about how much "whiter" or "lighter" they are going to be in the future; the children may simply be expressing their curiosity about the alternatives. Once a Black child understands race constancy, he or she will likely begin to make more positive statements about being Black.

Kenneth and Mamie Clark's pioneering studies from the late thirties and early forties, however, seemed to provide concrete evidence of self-hatred in Black children. The Clarks gave children as young as three, from both the North and the South, a choice of playing with a White doll or a Black doll. Regardless of geographic region, the Clarks found that Black children nearly always selected the White doll over the Black doll. Furthermore, when asked to explain their choices, the children said things like "The White doll seems nicer and prettier, with better coloring." The Clarks were later asked to appear before the U.S. Supreme Court to testify as expert witnesses about the damaging effects of educational segregation during the landmark 1954 case, *Brown* v. *Board of Education of Topeka, Kansas.* In *Simple Justice,* his book about the case, Richard Kluger cites

Kenneth Clark's description of the reactions of a participant in the doll study from South Carolina:

> Clark asked one dark brown girl of seven—"so dark she was almost black"—to take the coloring test that he generally gave along with the doll test. "When she was asked to color herself . . . she was one of the few children who picked a flesh color, pink, to color herself. When asked to color a little boy the color she liked little boys to be, she looked all around the twenty-four crayons and picked up a white crayon. . . ."

Although the Clarks' original research was later criticized on methodological grounds, in the late eighties, psychologist Michael Barnes replicated the original Clark doll test and discovered that nearly two-thirds of Black preschool children still chose White dolls over Black dolls. Barnes concluded that children, unlike adults, may be more honest about their racial self-hatred. Fortunately, such hatred can be unlearned—when he and his researchers spent several hours with the children discussing the positive aspects of being Black and then retested them, two-thirds chose the Black doll over the White.

In their own research with Black children, psychologists Darlene Powell-Hopson and her husband, Derek S. Hopson, drew similar conclusions. After asking Black preschoolers to choose between White and Black dolls, the researchers verbally praised those who had selected Black dolls, which they described as "pretty," "nice," "handsome," "clean," "smart," and "good." They also sent the children who had selected the White doll to the back of the class, while allowing the others to sit in the front. Fifteen minutes later, when the Hopsons retested the children, their preferences for the Black doll rose dramatically, from 35 percent to 71 percent.

Dr. Powell-Hopson currently serves as a consultant to Mattel Toys and has helped that company develop a special line of dolls for Black children. One doll, called Shani, the Swahili word for "marvelous," has dark skin, full lips, and a Negroid nose. Shani has two Black friends of different skin tones called Nichelle and Asha. Yet each of the new Black dolls has long hair flowing below the waist. More recently, Tyco Industries has introduced an African-American doll named Kenya. Her long, thick, curly hair can be straightened with a moisturizing solution or it can be styled in cornrows. Kenya comes with colored beads and a manual describing various ways to style her hair. It will be interesting to see what effects, if any, playing with such dolls will have on the future choices of African-American children given the Clark doll test.

A child's awareness and appreciation of the value of different skin colors occurs some time after racial awareness has developed. Some psychologists believe that Black children rarely use skin color as a criterion for racial grouping, but instead rely on facial features, eye color, and hair texture as indicators of Blackness. Other researchers think that children become more sensitive to skin-color variations as they become better able to extrapolate from information they have acquired about the world. For example, if a Black child gleans from fairy tales that only bad people and witches wear black and that heroes and fairy princesses are always dressed in white, the child may begin to reject other things that are black and dark, including himself. Some children are able to apply this kind of reasoning as early as age four, others around six or seven. In yet another replication of the doll test, psychologists George Gitter, David Mostofsky, and Yoichi Satow found in 1972 that dark-skinned Black children between the ages of four and six were more likely than those who were lighter to select White dolls when asked, "Which doll looks most like you?"

By the time they enter elementary school most children have learned to recognize certain subtleties of racial identity. Even so, some stumble over the word "Black." To young children, "black" is foremost a color, not an abstract racial category—and to be told that they are Black when they can see for themselves that they are not can be quite puzzling.

Katie K., the daughter of a Black man and a White woman in a predominantly White town in Minnesota, recalls having felt an intense confusion about race during her childhood. From the age of ten months, she was raised by a White family, who formally adopted her when she was two. These White parents tried to instill in her a strong sense of pride and self-esteem, and they told her at an early age not only that she was adopted but also, in the jargon of the early sixties, that she was a Negro. Just when Katie was starting to understand what it meant to be a Negro, the lexicon changed, and her parents told her she was Black. That made little sense to the five-year-old Katie, as she could see for herself that she was light skinned. One day when she was around seven she asked her mother, "Am I a nigger?" She had heard the word at school. Shocked, her mother exclaimed, "Don't ever say that again, Katie," leading Katie to conclude that she was not Black after all. For the next four or five years Katie was aware that she was different, but she was not sure how. It took her until she was eleven to figure it out, and some years more to reassess and accept her past confusion.

By the time they are teenagers, African-American children have well-defined stereotypes about skin color. Charles H. Parrish was one of the first to explore the nature of skin-color stereotyping in Black teenagers. He discovered in the 1940s that junior-high students used as many as 145 different terms to describe skin color, including "half-white," "yaller," "high yellow," "fair," "bright," "light," "red-bone," "light brown," "medium brown," "brown," "brownskin," "dark brown," "chocolate," "dark," "black," "ink spot," "blue black," and "tar baby." Each term was associated with a particular personality type: in general, light to medium skin tones were linked to intelligence and refinement, while dark skin tones suggested toughness, meanness, and physical strength.

Although Parrish's study is fifty years old, similar attitudes about skin color prevail among today's Black youth. Many believe that light skin is feminine and dark skin is masculine, and very light skinned boys and very dark skinned girls often suffer from being at odds with this cultural stereotype.

Some light-skinned Black males learn to compensate by exaggerating their masculinity, acting tough and streetwise. In an article in *Essence* entitled "Who Is Black," writer Itabari Njeri describes the plight of her cousin Jeffrey, who looked like singer Ricky Nelson but wanted to be "the baddest nigger on the block." Jeffrey died young on the streets trying to prove that he was not the enemy. And Michel Marriott, a reporter for the *New York Times,* recollects how, as a light-skinned Black youth coming of age during the sixties, "black cool dictated [his] every rhythm." Marriott's large Afro, his bodacious swagger, his white high-top Converse All-Stars, his obsession with knowing the latest Black music and dance moves, and his ability to cite Malcolm X flawlessly—all these traits articulated what his light skin never could, that he was a "bro-ske." As he wrote:

> A light-skinned teenager could not afford to get caught slipping when it came to the required black behavior [and] if you did you were very likely to get stoned with the hardest rock in a black teenager's rhetorical arsenal: Someone might call you a *whiteboy*.

Yet, says one brown-skinned corporate manager, a man named Ron Holt, once they outgrow adolescence light-skinned Black men are quick to realize the enormous advantages of their color. They discover that they have better job prospects, appear less threatening to Whites, and are more popular with women, who teasingly call them "pretty boys" or "run-round men." Many of them, never having fought harder to establish their Black identity, have a clearer sense of who they are as a result. Holt claims that it is the darker-skinned Black man, not his lighter-skinned brother, who is "Stepin Fetchitized" out of his masculinity. (Stepin Fetchit was an early Black film actor who always portrayed shuffling, laconic characters.)

For Black women, skin color is even more central to identity. Despite more than twenty years of "Black Is Beautiful" rhetoric, negative attitudes about women with dark skin persist. In a recent study at DePaul University in Chicago, Midge Wilson and two of her students, Lisa Razzano and Sherry Salmons, selected almost eighty people, evenly divided between males and females, Blacks and Whites, and asked them to look at photographs of twelve Black women and characterize their impressions of each. Regardless of the individual woman's attractiveness (prejudged to be high or low), the study participants nearly always rated the dark-skinned women as less successful, less happy in love, less popular, less physically attractive, less physically and emotionally healthy, and less intelligent than their light-skinned counterparts. The only quality in which the dark-skinned females were *not* rated lower was sense of humor, a phenomenon they labeled the "Whoopi Goldberg effect."

Certainly, the extent to which one can generalize from this research may be limited; everyone knows that first impressions, especially those formed from a photograph, are subject to change. Nonetheless, the halo that surrounds the light-skinned Black female may make it easier for her to form friendships and develop a positive sense of self, while dark-skinned females must work to overcome the negative stereotype. In fact, recent research by psychologist Cornelia Porter indicates that girls as young as six are twice as likely as boys to be sensitive to the social importance of skin color.

Black psychologist Maisha Bennett, who heads Maisha Bennett and Associates/Hamilton Behavioral Health Care in Chicago, conducts workshops for African-American women on self-esteem, relationships, and career development. She has found that in the safe atmosphere of a workshop Black women will discuss—often for the first time—their deepest fears about being "too light" or "too dark" or not having the "right" features. Some workshop participants may even discover that they have been using their skin color to distance themselves psychologically from others, in the same way that obese people sometimes use their weight to keep others at bay. While many Blacks can sympathize with those who are "too" dark skinned, fewer are willing to acknowledge the pain of those who are very light skinned, like the green-eyed, light-skinned Chicago woman who says that she has had people accuse her of being phony or of having a superiority complex simply because her skin is light and her eyes are not brown.

Dr. Tracy L. Robinson of North Carolina State University and Dr. Janie Victoria Ward of Simmons College have done studies showing that adolescents who are satisfied with their skin color are happiest with themselves and that those who believe that their skin is either too dark or too light are most likely to feel discontent. Robinson and Ward emphasize, however, that 80 percent of the adolescents they studied had high self-esteem. In fact, Ward found in another study that Black girls tend to have much higher self-esteem than White girls, perhaps because Black culture emphasizes independence and assertiveness in females.

A Haitian-born woman named Carolyn, dark-skinned with a strong and positive sense of self, realized back in grammar school that if someone was going to dislike her because of her color, then she did not want to be friends with that person anyway. It is a good lesson to learn early, and not just about color. Yet Carolyn has noticed that some dark-skinned Black women feel they must try harder to please others. She comments, "They're always getting their hair processed or wearing hair weaves or colored contact lenses." (Almost as an afterthought, Carolyn adds, "Black people don't seem to like each other very much.") Yet recent research by clinical psychologist Thomas Cash and his student Selena Bond found that darker-skinned African-American women were the most likely to select personal ideals of skin color in line with their own actual coloring. It was the medium-skinned Black women who tended to idealize skin tones lighter than their own, perhaps because for them, being just a little lighter was still within the realm of possibility. Regardless of their own satisfaction with their coloring, a full 70 percent of the Black women in the study believed that Black men preferred women whose skin was very light.

Distinctly Black first names can interact with skin color to convey certain social impressions. In another part of Midge's research using the twelve photographs of Black women, each participant was given a list of twenty-four feminine names and asked to guess which name belonged to which woman. Half of the names on the list were traditionally British or European, like Laura, Susan, and Diane; the others were stereotypically Black, like Lichelle, Sheronda, and Aretha. The darker the skin and the less attractive the woman, the more likely a participant was to assign her a stereotypically Black name. "Crazy names," as they are sometimes called within the Black community, are often linked to the bottom of the social hierarchy. A light-skinned Black woman named Dor-Tensia may be able to revel in her unusual name, but a darker-skinned Black woman may feel that her "crazy name," in concert with her dark skin, is just another sign that she is lower class.

One dark-skinned Black professional woman we interviewed believes that light-skinned women tend to have names with only one or two syllables, while dark-skinned women always have names with three or four syllables. Her hypothesis is unsubstantiated, but it does suggest that there may be others in the Black community who perceive a distinct relationship between skin color and first names.

In recent years, an increasing number of Black Americans have adopted African names. Itabari Njeri, in her book *Every Good-bye Ain't Gone,* describes some typical reactions to her new name.

> "What's your real name?"
>
> "Itabari Njeri is my real, legal name," I explain.
>
> "Okay, what's your original name?" they ask, often with eyes rolling, exasperation in their voices.
>
> After Malcolm X, Muhammad Ali, Kareem Abdul-Jabaar, Ntozake Shange and Kunta Kinte, who, I ask, should be exasperated by this question-and-answer game?
>
> Nevertheless, I explain, "Because of slavery, black people in the Western world don't usually know their original names. What you really want to know is what my slave name was."

The practice of claiming an African name began in the sixties as an expression of Black pride. The Nation of Islam advocated replacing one's last name with an X to symbolize the renunciation of the "master's" name inherited from enslaved ancestors. Taking a Muslim name, though, is different from taking a specifically African name. According to one orthodox Muslim, Jaleel Abdul-Adil, the Muslim name suggests a religious conversion rather than a cultural reclamation. "People bring a lot of assumptions to the table when they hear my name. Most think I'm a Black Nationalist, but Muslims embrace their culture within a spiritual context that affirms all races." The practice of taking African names seems to be on the rise again in the nineties, signaling a resurgence of ethnic pride.

Meanwhile, almost overnight "Black" has been declared too general, a term of racial designation that lacks cultural, historical, or political links to the "motherland," and "African American" has become the accepted label. Over the years, Blacks have been described in so many different ways—as "Negroes," "colored people," "persons of color," "colored Americans," "Black Anglo-Saxons," "Afro-Americans," "Afra-Americans," "black Americans," "Black Americans," "African Americans," and now, again, "persons of color"—that a sense of collective racial identity may have suffered in the process. African Americans may sound politically correct, but is it really the term preferred by those it describes? In a 1991 survey of 759 Black Americans, 72 percent reported that they still preferred to be called Black, while only 15 percent wanted to be called African American. The remaining 13 percent were undecided or preferred Afro-American or even Negro. These figures may reflect the fact that the use of African American is still new. Many who have been campaigning to replace Black with African American believe that Black only perpetuates a false racial category, while African American emphasizes cultural aspects of identity. Still, some members of the Black community dislike the new tag because it puts Africa before America, which is their most immediate homeland. In the words of a Black Chicago actor, Eric F.:

> The Black man and Black woman are still trying to define themselves in terms of Africa and I just find this almost ludicrous. Talk to an African, they don't think of us as part of them. They say your ancestors may have come from Africa, but it's obvious that *you* haven't. I think it's kind of futile to define yourselves in terms of Africa.

Finally, for some the label "African American" lacks emotional impact. As Katie K. put it, "Being Black speaks directly to my heart, while being African American speaks to my head."

During the sixties, slogans like "Black Power" and "I'm Black and I'm Proud" were the battle cries of an entire generation. Thousands of Black baby boomers can still recall the exact moment when they first proclaimed proudly, "I'm Black." Many directly credit James Brown and his hit song "I'm Black and I'm Proud" for their ability to "say it loud." During this extraordinary time—when dashiki-clad brothers and sisters took to the streets to safeguard their communities—being dark-skinned was finally in. When the sixties ended the concept of Black identity became less clear. Former Black radicals are now middle-aged, and some are solidly middle-class. A few even admit that they identify more closely with mainstream Whites than with their "brothers" and "sisters" in the underclass.

Deracination, the extent to which Blacks feel alienated from their African heritage as well as from other Blacks, is an important factor in Black identity. Because of the color gap in power and privilege, deracinated Blacks are more likely to have light skin than dark. Many grow up in predominantly White neighborhoods, attend predominantly White schools, and work in predominantly White businesses. They resent the fact that they are expected to "clean up the problems of the Black race." Some react in anger and embarrassment, instead of sympathy, when they witness other Blacks acting out negative stereotypes. Writer Joan Morgan, whose own family was not middle-class but striving hard for self-improvement as well as community improvement, confessed in an article in *Essence* to her own "better than thou" feelings on the subject.

Every time I hear African Americans speak horrid, broken English or I see a flash of gold teeth, public displays of Jheri-Curl* caps, genital-holding, or big, gold door-knocker earrings, I cringe. The hairs literally stand up on the back of my neck. I am fully aware that indulging in such obvious feelings of elitism is regressive and borders on identification with "the oppressor." I understand that, historically, politically and culturally, this system is designed for certain people to win and for others to lose. I acknowledge that my education—private schools and an Ivy League college—has placed me in a very privileged, winning position. But I can't help the way I feel.

Deracinated Blacks are referred to not only as "buppies" but also, more damningly, as "oreos"—chocolate on the outside and vanilla

---

*Jheri Curl, a type of "curl" manufactured by Jheri Redding, has become a widely used term for any kind of "curl."

on the inside. The concept is not unique to Blacks. Asians use "banana," Latinos use "coconut," and Native Americans use "apple" to describe those whose skin color disguises an inner Whiteness, that is, an alliance with the interests of the White majority.

Some deracinated Blacks with light-enough skin and keen-enough features have abandoned their heritage altogether, pretending to be White. Like deracination, the phenomenon of "passing" is hardly limited to African Americans—in Nazi Germany, Jews passed as Protestants; in today's army, gay men and women pass as straight; on job applications, older people try to pass as younger. In each case, the reason is traceable to some form of discrimination, be it on the basis of race, sexual orientation, or age.

Before the Civil War, passing was understandable, as it enabled Blacks to escape slavery and brutal racism. Today, passing is viewed with disdain by other Blacks, and while some African Americans pass "part-time" for economic reasons, by far the majority of those who could pass don't—and would never dream of doing so. Blacks who decide to pass for White pay a heavy price for their betrayal. They must renounce their heritage, terminate all contact with darker skinned relatives, and constantly monitor their speech patterns and social behavior. Many even forgo having children for fear a baby's color will blow their cover.

Yet there are many Blacks who pass without intending to. Thousands of light-skinned, fine-featured Blacks who identify themselves as Black are frequently mistaken for White. This can be a frustrating and emotionally exhausting experience. In *Who Is Black?*, F. James Davis discusses various responses to this kind of conflict: (1) hating all Whites; (2) reclaiming an African name or speaking with a distinctly Black accent; (3) dedicating oneself to public service and the elimination of all forms of discrimination; (4) serving as a liaison between the White and Black communities; (5) avoiding issues of racial identity altogether, focusing instead on some other aspect of identity, such as that derived from work.

One inadvertent "passer," Kathleen Cross, has blended several of Davis's strategies. The daughter of a White woman and a Black man, Cross wears T-shirts emblazoned with the statement "Before

There Was Any History There Was Black History.'' She has confronted both color and race discrimination in appearances on the *Donahue Show,* and in an article in *Ebony* she has discussed not only the pain but also the privilege she has incurred from being trapped in a White woman's body.

> For some reason, contrary to genetic odds, the only pigment God saw fit to give me was in the freckles which he sprinkled across my face. My skin, my hair, my features are White, but my experience is not. Neither is it wholly Black. . . . Although my skin color has often shielded me from being the target of White racism, it has also created for me one of the most painful of human conditions, a lifetime of being misperceived and initially rejected by my own people. This is not an indictment; it is simply a testimonial to the remnants of White racism that have divided, and continue to divide, the descendants of Africa in America.

Some Whites cannot understand people like Kathleen Cross. They wonder why she does not use the ''eyeball test'' and just declare herself White, or they doubt the sincerity of her claim to Black identity. After all, there are few advantages associated with being Black in America. Although Cross does not believe she must denounce her European heritage in favor of an African one, many people still question what motivates her commitment to being African American.

The answer to all these questions is rooted in the one-drop rule of racial identity, which, more than any other factor, has shaped the development of racial identity in America. Although it had its origin in racism, today the rule is staunchly defended by most members of the Black community. By definition, the one-drop rule unites all those with Black ancestry. It enables the Black community to draw on the leadership of its lighter-skinned members, who often have more credibility with Whites. It strengthens a sense of racial loyalty that discourages members from passing as White or marrying outside the race. Charles Stewart, a speaker at the 1990 convention of the National Association of Black Journalists, neatly summed up the advantages of the one-drop rule by asking all those in attendance who considered themselves Black to raise their hands. A majority of the audience did. Stewart next requested a show of hands by all those who considered themselves pure African. Not a single hand went up. Stewart's pointed conclusion: "We cannot afford to have an empty room."

But a growing number of biracial and multicultural Americans are actively challenging this kind of thinking. Playwright Velina Hasu Houston, the executive director of the Amerasian League, is the daughter of a Japanese mother and a father of mixed Indian and Black ancestry. Houston recalls the way her father explained her racial identity.

> When I was four years old, I went into the kitchen of my home and I said to my mother, "Mommy, why are you va-nilla and why is Papa chocolate?" And my father went out and bought a carton of Neapolitan ice cream and he came back and he said, "You see this chocolate stripe? You see this red stripe? That's me." And he cut it into the bowl. And then he said, "Do you see this vanilla stripe? That's your mother." And he mixed it up in the bowl. He showed me the brown mixture and he said, "You see? That's you and your sister." And I said, "Yes." And he said, "Now, can you take that out and put it back into the three stripes?" I said, "No, I can't."

Today, Houston, like thousands of other multicultural Americans, refuses to deny the individual parts of her self. She identifies herself as Black, but because her mother instilled in her an appreciation of Japanese culture she also considers herself Asian American. Some Blacks have angrily accused her of being ashamed of her Blackness. Others claim she is denying the fact that, no matter what she may think of herself, others will see her only as Black. She firmly maintains that no one else can determine her racial identity for her.

Because Velina's mother was Japanese, she probably learned more about her Asian heritage than if her father were Japanese and her mother were African American. In most societies, ethnic and family culture is transmitted through the mother. As a result, Black-White biracial children whose mothers are Black may find it easier to conform to societal expectations of their racial identity than those whose mothers are White. When a White mother informs her racially mixed children that they are Black, she must renounce her own Whiteness—a phenomenon that biracial advocates label the ''White mother martyr syndrome''—and this can lead to adjustment problems in her children. A White woman named Anne (not her real name) has talked about the way she and her Black husband agreed to handle the issue: since society would consider their two light-skinned, gray-eyed sons Black, she would not confuse them by telling them otherwise. Still, there were problems. She recalls that when her younger son, at the age of ten, asked about his race, she told him, ''You're Black.'' But then he asked, ''Well, what are you?'' When Anne replied, ''I am White,'' he angrily retorted, ''If you're White, then why do I have to be Black? Am I not good enough to be what you are?'' At the time all Anne could think to say was, ''I'm sorry, son, but that's just the way it is.'' Now in his twenties, her son still seems resentful of Anne for not allowing him to be part of who she is.

Both within their families and outside of them, biracial persons often feel alienated and confused. Advocates of multiethnic and biracial identity sometimes receive harsh treatment from the larger Black community, and in response many have formed their own support groups. One such group is the Biracial Family Network of Chicago, a nonprofit organization headed by Ramona Douglass, who speaks for many others when she emphasizes that racial identity is a matter of personal choice. Similarly, she rejects the notion that a person who has claimed to be multiracial cannot also be Black. ''Simply because I am multiethnic doesn't mean I am saying I am not a person of color,'' Ramona says, adding, ''It doesn't mean that I won't fight for civil rights.''

Carlos Fernandez, president of the Association of Multi Ethnic Americans (AMEA), which is based in San Francisco, also rejects the notion that you have to sacrifice one race to claim another. He points out that those who insist that the multiethnic movement will undermine the efforts of other minorities are basing their fears on misconceptions about current antidiscrimination law. To the very small extent that antidiscrimination programs require the hiring of minorities in proportion to their numbers in the regional population (which usually only happens as the result of a lawsuit to correct a pattern of blatant discrimination), those who choose to disqualify themselves from the counting of a particular minority because they are multiethnic will disqualify themselves from the benefits of the program as well. There is no danger that members of a disadvantaged minority would find themselves with fewer jobs available just because multiethnic individuals have placed themselves in another category. Moreover, Fernandez adds, "those who have studied the history of race relations in the United States have long noted that traditionally White racism has provided greater opportunities for lighter-skinned multiracial individuals. Compared to 'monoracial' minorities, lighter-skinned individuals have actually had greater socioeconomic success. It is even possible that such persons have actually benefited disproportionately from antidiscrimination and affirmative action programs, although the evidence for this is less clear." Fernandez also points out that in addition to economic questions, the complex web of issues surrounding multiethnicity involves political questions such as the gerrymandering of districts by race: "Is it really proper to count people who are mixed race as monoracial? Should we have districts for mixed races? If multiethnic people are to be included in minority benefit programs, should they be considered under a separate category? As long as we ignore the fact of multiethnicity in America, we cannot answer such important questions." Like an increasing number of Americans, Fernandez finds the construct of "race" itself outmoded, the residue of a nineteenth-century obsession with "scientific" categories. "As far as I'm concerned, 'racist' means thinking about people in terms of categories of race," Fernandez says.

Some determined multiethnic persons are refusing to check a single box for "race" on forms and applications, knowing full well that the computer will "kick out" their multiple responses. They are also challenging the allocation of only one racial category to African Americans on U.S. census forms, while Asian Americans have nine.

In the 1990 census, 9.8 million Americans of mixed Hispanic, Asian, African, or European blood checked "other" to describe their racial identity, a 45 percent increase from 1980. While most of those who checked "other" were of Hispanic descent, a growing number of individuals of African ancestry are also beginning to embrace their multiethnic identity.

Dr. Barbara Love of the University of Massachusetts believes that racial identity in America is sociopolitical, not biological or genetic. According to Love, racial categories, while clarifying nothing, perpetuate a system of privilege based on race. "Our goal should be fewer racial categories, not more," she says, "until race has lost its power to predict privilege."

Multiethnic celebrities have learned just how political their choices of identity can be, especially if several groups want to claim them as their own. Actress Jasmine Guy, star of the television series *A Different World,* has a Black father and a White mother and refers to herself proudly as African American. She has said that although she had a few "where do I fit in" problems while growing up, basically she has always known that she was Black. Jennifer Beals, who starred in the hit movie *Flashdance,* asserts that she is neither Black nor White and marks "other" on applications. Renee Tenison, the first "Black" woman to be *Playboy*'s "Playmate of the Year," believes that "if you have one-quarter of Black in you, people feel you should deny anything else in you, and that's not fair. I am White, too. My mother is White." And Paula Abdul, whose mother is French-Canadian and whose father is Brazilian-Syrian, calls herself neither White nor Black but Third World—a position that has angered some Black American fans. Each of these four women expresses her racial identity differently, and each has met with criticism.

The United States has no legal concept of biraciality. Depending on the state, biracial offspring automatically acquire the race of either the mother, the father, the minority parent, or the Black parent according to the traditional one-drop rule. Although a few states, like Hawaii, do not adhere strictly to the one-drop rule, no state takes into consideration an infant's physical appearance, and none gives adults the right to change their original race designation, even if they feel they have been categorized incorrectly.

In 1983, the case of a Louisiana woman named Susie Phipps exemplified the absurdity of the one-drop rule. Although Phipps looked White, was raised as White, and identified herself as White, a midwife had designated her "Colored" on her birth certificate. In 1770, Phipps's White great-great-great-great-grandfather had had a slave mistress, and the midwife in the small community where Phipps was born apparently knew that some of her ancestors and relatives, including her parents, were considered Colored. When, as an adult, Phipps declared herself White on her application for a passport, the discrepancy was discovered and the passport denied. Phipps sued. While ultimately the case helped to liberalize the definition of racial identity in the state of Louisiana, the courts denied Phipps's appeal, and she remained legally Black. (Interestingly, state governments are more willing to grant applicants the right to change their race from White to Black than vice versa—an inherently racist double standard.)

In response to this kind of logic, one might ask (as the author and music critic Gene Lees has in his *Jazzletter*), "Is Black blood so strong and White blood so weak, that an ounce of the former is capable of wiping out generations of the latter?"

Personal identity is private and mysterious. Psychologists still do not know what causes a homosexual identity to emerge, much less a racial identity. We do know, however, that among people who are biracial, those who experience the greatest difficulties in adjustment and who suffer the most from their marginal status are those whose physical features are at odds with their inner sense of self—that is, individuals with dark skin and African features who feel White and those with light skin and White features who consider themselves Black. Clearly, societal racism makes it difficult to acquire a positive sense of racial pride, but the one-drop rule also plays a role. Not every person with a degree of Black blood is going to feel 100 percent Black, nor, perhaps, should everyone who wants to identify as White be charged with the "crime" of passing. Biracial advocate

Ramona Douglass astutely observes that the concept of "passing" is itself racist in origin. It is her contention that if the concept is to be applied consistently, then someone who is genetically more White than Black could be accused of "passing" for Black.

Historically, the one-drop rule has both helped and harmed the Black community. While increasing its numbers, the rule has fractured the community's solidarity. In so broadly defining a genetically varied population with a wide range of features and skin colors, the rule has created a race grouping more social than biological. Nowhere else in the world does a single race encompass people whose skin color ranges from white to black, whose hair texture varies from tightly curled to straight, and whose facial features reflect the broadest possible diversity. Were it not for this artificial grouping, part of the legacy of racism, Blacks might not criticize each other so harshly for having skin or hair that does not meet some arbitrary standard.

5. Hair: The Straight and Nappy of It All

*As the twentieth century closes, I believe that Black women
have come to better appreciate the array of beauty we portray,
despite subtle, and not so subtle, pressure from the media,
the workplace and the larger society to conform to their standards
of attractiveness.*

*Yet I am sometimes troubled that too many of us still
make snide and cruel comments about the politically,
professionally or socially acceptable way to wear our hair.
We would be a lot stronger as a people if we used
that energy to support each other economically, emotionally
and spiritually.*

—A'LELIA PERRY BUNDLES,
Great-great-granddaughter of
Madam C. J. Walker,
Black hair care industry pioneer

A half-dozen Black women vied for space in front of the restroom
mirror, retouching their makeup and spraying their hair. One of them,
whose hair was short and nappy, inquired of no one in particular,
"What is this mass of sheep's wool that sits so prominently atop our
heads? What did Black people do to deserve this bad-ass hair from
hell?"

A light-skinned woman whose long hair was casually pulled up
in a ponytail answered, "Oh, girl, stop taking your hair so damned
seriously. It's just hair." And another dark-skinned sister with a short,
kinky hairstyle interjected, "Sure, you can say that because you got
'good' hair, and ain't nobody ever called you no bald-headed bitch."
During the shouting and name-calling that ensued no one bothered
to ask, "Why does it matter so much?" Perhaps the answer is too

obvious. As Susan Brownmiller wrote, in *Femininity,* "Hair indeed may be trivial, but it is central to the feminine definition."

Embodying some Black women's worst fears, a working-class Black man named Darryl describes a far too popular formula for weighing the beauty of Black women in the following words:

> If a Black woman is light-skinned with good hair and good features, then she's the shit. Even if she has short hair, but good features, she'll be all right. But a dark-skinned girl with short hair can forget it. And if she has a big nose, then she should just be a nun. But if she has long hair and good features, then her skin color can be overlooked. Long hair really helps out those black ugly girls.

The politics of hair parallels the politics of skin color. Among Black women, straight hair and European hairstyles not only have been considered more feminine but have sent a message about one's standing in the social hierarchy. "Good hair" has long been associated with the light-skinned middle class, "bad hair" with Blacks who are less fortunate.

The sixties marked a revolution in Blacks' attitudes about their hair; for the first time young women in significant numbers stopped perming and processing, and members of both sexes let their hair grow wild and free in the style known as the Afro. But when the sixties ended, and the 'fro was no longer fashionable, the old attitudes about hair quickly resurfaced. The tradition of calling hair that was straight and wavy "good" and hair that was tightly curled and nappy "bad" had never really gone away. Men like Darryl continued to evaluate Black women according to what was on their heads instead of what was in them, and the self-confidence of many Black women continued to hinge on the freshness of their perms.

In this post-sixties era, hair remains a politically charged subject. To some, how an African American chooses to style his or her hair says everything there is to be said about that individual's Black consciousness, socioeconomic class, and probable life-style, particularly when the individual is a woman.

Clearly, hair is less an issue for men than for women. Beginning in childhood, boys conventionally wear short hair while girls grow their hair long. Adult Black males generally keep their hair cropped short, so its texture is usually not that important to them. But from an early age most Black girls, especially those with fuzzy edges and nappy "kitchens" (the hairline at the back of the neck), are taught to "fix" their hair—as if it were broken. Short hair is unfeminine but for many long hair is unmanageable. Still the hair of Black girls is braided and yanked, rubber-banded and barretted, into a presentable state. And when mothers grow weary of taming their daughters' hair, many opt to treat it with chemical relaxers. As one Black mother tired of fighting the comb declared, "I didn't have time to mess with that child's nappy head any longer, so I went and got it permed. It's been a lot easier on both of us since."

Some Black women come to regret what was done to their hair as children. A woman named Yvette longingly remembers what her hair was like when she was young. She says that many of her earliest memories feature her Afro-puffs (hair that is parted in the middle, rubber-banded, and "picked out" into two small Afros, one on each side) or her thousand braids with bows at the end. She also remembers how fascinated the White children at school were by the natural softness of her hair and how they were always asking to touch it. "For me, my hair was a source of pride and uniqueness," she recalls. But as she neared adolescence her mother declared that she "was turning into a young lady" and it was time for her first permanent relaxer. Today, in her thirties, Yvette yearns for her natural hair, yet she continues to get permanents regularly. "In order to reverse the process now, it would mean a lot of hair breakage and hair loss," she sighs. "At this point in my life, it's a lot less effort just to deal with it the way it is." (The place where permed hair meets virgin hair is often weak and keeping the hair permed may actually prevent further breakage.)

For many other Black women, childhood memories of short, nappy locks bring forth feelings of shame, not sweet nostalgia. A dark-skinned woman named Caroline remembers other children's taunts of "Your hair's so short, you can smell yo' brains." Caroline was ecstatic when her mother marched her down to Sister Westbury's Beauty Nook for her first perm.

> I had it doubly hard when I was in grade school. Not only was I dark-skinned but I also had short beady hair. I always got teased by the boys and laughed at by the girls because my hair was so nappy and always stuck up in the air. I hated my hair and cried many nights. I was so glad when I got my hair straightened. It changed my whole life.

Many young Black girls view their first perm as a rite of passage, and sometimes it is their parents, particularly those who grew up in the sixties, who are sorry when a daughter stops going natural. In an article entitled "Life with Daughters or The Cakewalk with Shirley Temple," Gerald Early, a professor of English and African-American studies at Washington University, described his intense disappointment the day his two daughters, aged seven and ten, came home with their hair permed.

> During that summer the girls abandoned their Afro hairstyles for good. When they burst through the door with their hair newly straightened, beaming, I was so taken aback in a kind of horror that I could only mutter in astonishment when they asked, "How do you like it?"
>
> It was as if my children were no longer mine, as if a culture that had convinced them they were ugly had taken them from me. The look I gave my wife brought this response from her: "They wanted their hair straightened, and they thought they were old enough for it. Besides, there is no virtue in wearing an Afro. I don't believe in politically correct hair."

Yet for Black women hair *is* political, and those who are "happy nappy" consider perming "politically incorrect," just as others consider unstraightened hair a disgrace. No matter which choice a Black woman makes, someone may react negatively to it.

On a vacation trip to British Virgin Gorda, the Black poet, essayist, and writer Audre Lorde discovered just how easily her hairstyle could be interpreted politically. Wearing newly fashioned dreadlocks (a style in which the hair is either braided, twisted, or clumped together in separate strands all over the head), Lorde arrived at the Beef Island Airport and was told by the immigration officer—a Black woman with heavily processed hair—that her entry was being denied. Angry at the snag in her travel plans, Lorde demanded to speak to the woman's supervisor and was informed that her dreadlocks marked her as a dope-smoking Rastafarian revolutionary. Fortunately, the officer was eventually able to determine that Lorde was not a "dangerous" Rastafarian, and her passport was stamped "admit."

But unprocessed hair may also elicit political approval. Mary Morten, a former president of the Chicago chapter of the National Organization for Women, who keeps her hair in a short natural style, remembers the time a Black man came running up to her on the street holding a rolled-up poster. He said, "I've been waiting for a sister with natural hair so I can give her this poem." When Morten unfurled the poster, she found printed on it a Gwendolyn Brooks poem. She was so touched by the message and by the way it came to her that she hung the poster on the wall of the Chicago NOW office. The poem reads:

TO THOSE OF MY SISTERS
WHO KEPT THEIR NATURALS
        Never to look
        a hot comb in the teeth.

   Sisters!
   I love you
   Because you love you.
. . . .
You have not bought Blondine.
You have not hailed the hot-comb recently.
You never worshipped Marilyn Monroe.
You say: Farrah's hair is hers

You have not wanted to be white.
Nor have you testified to adoration of that state
with the advertisement of imitation,
(never successful because the hot comb is laughing too.)

But oh the rough rough Other music.
the Real,
the Right.
the natural Respect for self and seal.
     Sisters!
Your hair is Celebration in the world.

Nonetheless, Black women who wear their hair unprocessed are often squawked at, teased, and harassed. One sister with long brown dreadlocks says, ''When my hair was going through the 'wile chile' stage [the first phase of growing dreadlocks, in which the hair looks completely untamed], a brother actually stopped me on the street demanding to know 'when in the hell' was I going to 'do somethin' with my nappy-headed ass hair.' '' The award-winning actress Whoopi Goldberg often has members of her own community tell her that her dreadlocks are disgusting and that she should ''take those nappy braids out.'' A generation earlier, the actress Cicely Tyson was told by members of the Black community that she might be a gifted actress but her short natural hairstyle was detrimental to the image of Black women.

Although political reasons for sporting European-looking hairstyles abound, some Black women relax their hair just because they like it that way. One of them, a woman named Catherine, who owns a small business, says that she loves her hair long and would never consider cutting it.

My long hair is my best feature. I realize it's high maintenance but I'd much rather get up an hour early and do my hair than to have short hair. There's something special about Black women with long hair.

A certain level of Black consciousness would seem to be necessary before a woman dares to go natural. The relationship between hairstyle and politics is far from clear, however. One African-American professional woman from Chicago has said that she could not imagine wearing her hair in any way but dreadlocks, or perhaps cornrows, since everything she does emanates from an Afrocentric perspective. Yet she admits to knowing women as strongly Afrocentric as she who routinely process their hair, and others with no interest at all in fostering Black culture or politics who wear natural styles like cornrows.

Dreadlocking perhaps carries a more radical political connotation than any other hairstyle. Yet all it entails is growing curly hair out to the point where it "locks," the stage at which dreadlocks become permanent and cannot be changed without cutting. Few Whites have hair curly enough to grow into "dreads"; with rare exceptions, the style is uniquely Black. Traditionally, dreadlocks have been associated with the Rastafarians of Jamaica, and American men with dreadlocks are usually musicians or members of the counterculture. However, an increasing number of American Black women are adopting the style. They are writers and performers, like Alice Walker and Whoopi Goldberg, or professors, journalists, and social workers—not exactly corporate types, but not members of a counterculture, either.

Dark-skinned Black women who grow dreadlocks appear to have reached a point in their lives at which they no longer feel the need to compensate for the color of their skin. Breaking free of all their past conditioning about hair may be part of a larger spiritual awakening. After being criticized by a "bro" for wearing her hair in dreads, one brown-skinned woman commented, "It's too bad Black men don't see the beauty and the spirituality of my hair." Sandra B., who manages an urban charity organization in Chicago, also describes her dreadlocks in spiritual terms.

I love my hair like this. I wouldn't trade it for straight hair any day. There is something so spiritual and in-touch about my hair. I feel connected with my roots. My hair gives me a sense of oneness with nature. You know how beautiful nature is when it's just left alone to grow naturally the way God intended? Well, that's how I look at my hair. Just growing naturally the way God intended.

Freelance writer Naadu Blankson, in an article in *Essence,* has compared the unlocking of her inhibitions with the dreadlocking of her hair, and Alice Walker once wrote, in the same magazine, that the ability to "lock" may depend on the flow of one's natural energy not being blocked by "anger, hatred, or self-condemnation."

There are many misconceptions about dreadlocks, and those who wear them must answer a lot of questions, many of them from members of their own community. The most common include: "Can you wash your hair that way?" (yes); "Does it smell?" (no more than anyone else's); "If you want to change it, must you shave it off and begin anew?" (most likely); "How do you get your hair to do that?" (it just does it on its own). One woman who got tired of the constant inquiries tells how she turns the tables on the questioner.

When Black people ask me what I did to my hair, I tell them, I haven't done anything to my hair. The question is, especially for those who have Jheri Curls, what have *you* done to *your* hair. Unlike you, I wash my hair all the time, and when I get up in the morning I don't have stains on my pillow.

Simone Hylton, an Afrocentric beautician, believes that most Black women are misinformed about what is good and bad for their hair. Many assume that dreadlocking is harmful, yet few know just how much damage constant processing can do. According to Hylton, Black hair is not as fragile as is commonly thought. Straightening, chemical relaxing, and frequent washing burn the scalp and cause hair breakage; dreadlocking does not. "Look at people who wear dreads; their hair is long. If you wore dreads for ten years, your hair would grow past your butt, too."

When a Black woman comes to Hylton with hair damaged by years of perming, she sometimes has to cut off all the permed growth. If the woman still wants long hair, Hylton will braid extensions onto what remains, to give the hair a rest and help restore it to its natural state.

In the politically charged world of hairstyling, Hylton has even come under fire for weaving these extensions into hair—her own hair as well as that of her clients. Hylton, who wears a Senegalese twist (a style in which the hair is twisted into ringlets, sometimes with African linen intertwined), has this response to such criticism:

> Weaving extensions into the hair originated in Africa. Members of different tribes would take plants and weave them into their hair. Weaving or twisting isn't done just to get length. It's an art form and a part of African culture.

Black women with long hair, whether natural or processed, whether achieved by hair weaves or extensions, are acutely sensitive to accusations that they are trying to look White. Like Hylton, they often draw on ancient customs to defend their choices. When asked about the melange of long braids neatly twisted into a hair weave hanging down her back, Pamela, a Black graduate student in psychology, replied without missing a beat.

> I wear my hair like this for a reason. It's convenient and I feel very attractive. My ancestors from Egypt wore their hair long and straight or braided. Sometimes both. This is not about having long hair to try to be White; this is about being who I am as an African American. It has more to do with style and cosmetics than it has to do with being like some White woman. My hair is an accessory.

Black hairstylist Nantil Chardonnay, of Nantil for Egypt III Hair Salon, maintains that virtually all of today's popular hairstyles can be traced to early African cultures. But she laments that it has usually taken a White woman—like Bo Derek with her braids in the 1980 hit film *10*—to popularize, even among Blacks, what has been a traditionally African hairstyle. Although some Black women in the sixties and seventies were wearing beaded braids and cornrows as an expression of their African heritage, this was not considered a mainstream thing to do within the Black community until after *10* came out. In Chardonnay's words, "I thought it was very shallow of them [African-American women] suddenly to want to copy someone else who was copying our culture to begin with."

Hair texture, like skin tone, carries much social and historical baggage for Blacks. All things being equal, a Black woman whose hair grows naturally straight is usually thought to be from a "better" family than a woman whose hair is very nappy. Black women who wear natural styles, like braids, cut across socioeconomic lines, but a politically defiant style like dreadlocks is generally a middle-class expression of Black consciousness. Inner-city girls and women are probably the least likely to wear dreadlocks. Poor Black women with very kinky hair strive instead for straighter-looking hair, but because they cannot afford constant professional relaxation treatments (which can cost up to $85 a session), their hair often looks stiff and overly processed, in what is derisively called a "ghetto 'do." Still, hair is so important to Black women that, regrettably, some would rather be late paying their rent than miss getting their hair permed.

But the split between Black women who process and those who do not is not as great or malevolent as Spike Lee's *School Daze*—in which the men debate politics and the women fight about their skin color and hair—might lead one to think. In *School Daze* women with light skin and straight hair are derisively called "Wannabees," and dark-skinned women are "Jigaboos." Their big dance number takes place in Madam Re-Re's beauty parlor. There, among the hair dryers and chemical relaxers, the Black coeds sing a lively number called "Straight and Nappy." It opens with a spate of vicious name-calling between the two groups of women.

Wannabees: Pick-a-ninny
Jigaboos: Barbie Doll, High Yella Heffer
W: Tarbaby
J: Wanna be White
W: Jig-a-boo

Chorus: Talkin' 'bout good and bad hair
   whether you are dark or fair
   go on and swear
   see if I care
   good and bad hair. . . .
  W: Your hair ain't no longer than (*finger snap*)
   so you'll never fling it all back
   and you 'fraid to walk in the rain
   oh, what a shame, who's to blame
  J: Don't you ever worry 'bout that
   'cause I don't mind being BLACK
   go on with your mixed-up head
   I ain't gonna never be 'fraid
  W: Well you got nappy hair
  J: Nappy is all right with me
  W: My hair is straight you see
  J: But your soul's crooked as can be. . . .

Although many thought that *School Daze* was demeaning to Black women, Lee did inject some humor into the hair issue—doubtless a good thing in the long run.

While African Americans assign the hair issue various degrees of political weight, most Black women, whether they process or not, respect and understand the choices of others. There is, after all, a reality factor to contend with in White-dominated America. For example, a Black teacher from California who had been content with wearing her hair in a natural decided to straighten it when she and her husband began to look for a house to buy.

While more and more Black women today are daring to go natural, they remain a distinct minority. Straightened hair is the standard for "respectable" Black women—those with corporate careers as well as the wives of Black politicians and businessmen. An estimated 75 percent of American Black women continue to perm or relax their hair.

In all fairness, some Black women simply look better with their hair processed, and those who want to wear it that way have as much right to do so as Whites. As one Black sister puts it, "White people don't have a patent on long hair."

Meanwhile, in the nineties short styles are suddenly "in." From the boyish (but processed-looking) haircuts of the "Uh Huh" girls of the Diet Pepsi commercials to the closely cropped natural locks of Black actress Halle Berry *(Jungle Fever, Boomerang),* the traditional view that long hair is sexier seems to be changing. Berry says that she loves her short hair: "I feel people see me now. I will never grow my hair long again!"

Still, some Black women (and White women, too) say they continue to keep their hair long because that is what they think men prefer. A Black college student named Crystal says that when her boyfriend saw her getting her hair cut short, he walked out at the first snip and would not talk to her for two weeks. But it is hard to generalize: another Black man, an electrical engineer from the Chicago area, says that he is partial to Black women who wear their hair short and natural: "There's something so pure and genuine about these women," while another man counters, "Brothers like their women with long hair so they can grab hold of it during sex."

Sometimes the very men who like long hair tell their women not to "wear that arsenal [rollers] to bed," and then in the morning ask, "Why is your hair sticking up all over your head?" Fortunately, in this feminist era, a growing number of Black women are choosing to wear their hair in styles that please themselves first, not their men. At the same time, more African-American men are beginning to experiment with different hairstyles of their own. In the process, they may be becoming more tolerant and perhaps more sensitive to the difficulties of constant hair maintenance.

One currently popular Black men's hairstyle is the "high-top fade," popularized by the rapper Kid of *Kid N' Play* (who also starred in *House Party).* Short on the sides, long and flat on top, it goes by other names, including "wedge," "slant," "Philly fade," "gumbie," "low 'n' tight," or just "big hair." Like other inner-city trends, including ripped jeans and earrings on men, the fade appears to be making its way into mainstream culture. Modified versions of it are even cropping up on the heads of middle-class men, Black and White.

Another male street hairstyle, this one with roots in Africa, entails shaving a pattern through the hair so that the scalp shows through. Some Black youths have even taken to shaving their favorite logos, like Nike, onto the back of their heads. Like the Afro of the sixties, these radical razor designs are an artistic expression of Black culture. But these styles are also faddish and are already losing favor in some urban areas.

While hairstyle has never been a central part of the color complex in perceptions of Black men, certain 'dos are associated with certain life-styles. In the nineties, Black men who texturize their hair are usually entertainers—musicians, television celebrities, big-name athletes—although a few Black businessmen have experimented with hair relaxers to improve their corporate image. The more radical styles, like razor cuts, dreadlocks, and extreme high-top fades, are avoided by Black businessmen, just as very long hair and punk cuts are avoided by White businessmen who want the establishment to take them seriously.

In general, Black men seem to have a more positive attitude toward their hair than most Black women do. Even when they start to go bald, they can shave it all off, as the Chicago Bulls basketball star Michael Jordan does, and make a fashion statement.

Meanwhile, anguished concerns about hairstyles have hurt and held back Black women, and, as the quotation by A'Lelia Bundles implies, women must, together, begin to move beyond such concerns. Shameful attitudes about hair often begin at home. Within the family, Black parents need to teach their sons and daughters that though hair comes in a variety of textures, there is no such thing as good or bad hair. If you got hair, good!

6. Divided Families and Friends

*. . . And over and over, from the little crowd about the bassinet came
those shrills and sprightly observations, "Why that child's got his father's
nose and mouth, and good hair! Course Anna Bella's got good hair,
just look at that pretty child!" And what if it had gone another way,
Anna Bella thought. It seemed it was all that concerned them, that mixture
of the white and black, could this child perhaps pass?*
—ANNE RICE,
The Feast of All Saints

This scene from Anne Rice's novel is set in nineteenth-century Louisiana, but similar scenes are still common at the birth of children
today. Many Black families can barely disguise their anxious concern
about the color and features of a newborn. Following routine inquiries about a baby's sex, weight, and health, most relatives will immediately want to know, "What's he [or she] look like?"—a veiled
request for information about skin color and features. Family members are likely to be intensely curious about the children of parents
with very different skin tones, and especially those of different racial
backgrounds; early reactions may range from "Look at that little yella
thing" to "You better keep that child out of the sun." Such comments, first from family members and later from friends and peers,
shape the psychology of a Black child as it grows from infancy to
adulthood.

In her book *Black Families in Therapy*, psychologist Nancy Boyd-
Franklin has identified unique stresses that arise from the issue of
skin color. Afrocentric parents may view a child with light skin as an
ugly reminder of their slave heritage and may blame the child for not
looking Black enough. In his autobiography, Malcolm X describes
how his light skin displeased his mother, since she was ashamed of

her White father. Other families may "scapegoat" dark-skinned children and pamper those who are light, as sociologist Elliot Liebow discusses in his book *Tally's Corner*. While most African-American family members do not dwell obsessively on differences in color, rarely is the subject neutral or unmentioned.

Obsession with color may begin even before the child's birth. Sandra Braine, the program director of a clinic that provides social services to pregnant girls fourteen and younger, says that most of the pregnant Black girls she has counseled fantasize about having babies with light skin, light eyes, and "good" hair. And when a girl who has given birth comes back to the clinic with her baby for a visit, the pregnant girls gather around to "oooh" and "aaah" if the baby is light skinned, but practically ignore the mother and child if the baby is dark skinned.

The pregnant Black girls who most intensely desire lighter-skinned babies are nearly always those who have lighter-skinned mothers, many of whom were ashamed that their daughters were dark. These girls have grown up hearing comments like "Get your nappy-headed ass outta here" or "How many times do I have to call your Black ass?" and consequently have developed intense inferiority complexes. Some confess to having intentionally gotten pregnant by a light-skinned boy in the hope that a light-skinned baby would finally bring them love, from their mothers as well as their babies. One Black nurse recalls the look of dismay on the face of one dark-skinned young woman after the birth of the baby she had conceived with a Puerto Rican boyfriend. Like most newborns, the infant was fairly light skinned, but when the young mother inspected its genitals, earlobes, and knuckles for clues to the child's mature color, she cried, "Oh, my God, my baby has been touched by the tar brush!"

Black children quickly absorb the guilt, anger, jealousy, and depression generated in their families by an unresolved color complex. A woman we'll call Rachel, the eldest—and by far the lightest—of the four children of a very light skinned mother and a dark-skinned father in Georgia, was coddled by her parents because of her color. As a result, her younger siblings came to hate her, and one sister in particular acted out her resentment by slashing Rachel's clothes and, once, cutting off her long hair while she slept. Her parents made the situation worse by punishing the dark-skinned daughter and consoling the fair-skinned Rachel. Eventually her father left, and her mother invited a darker-skinned sister to live with the family. The aunt, who had always resented her own lighter-skinned sister, began to pick on Rachel, hissing, "Stop flipping your hair like a White girl—you've always wanted to be a White girl, you little bitch." Rachel, now in her twenties, still feels anxious and insecure whenever she happens to toss her hair. She is gaining confidence, however, from working with a Black therapist who zeroed in almost immediately on Rachel's deep-seated complex about color—something that her previous therapist, who was White, had not explored.

Even in families where color does not seem to be much of an issue, siblings learn to use their differences as ammunition in ordinary rivalries. Joni, a light-skinned woman, remembers that calling her still lighter-skinned sister "a green-eyed bitch" inevitably sent her into a frenzy of rage. In healthy families, such sibling conflict may actually relieve pent-up feelings and make the whole issue seem less serious or threatening. It is when color remains an unspoken concern that children may suffer the most.

In her book *Balm in Gilead*, Sara Lawrence Lightfoot, a Black Harvard sociologist, recounted her own family's struggle with color, focusing in the following paragraph on the experiences of her mother, the psychiatrist Dr. Margaret Morgan Lawrence.

They were a handsome family. Margaret's memory of them comes around—as it so often does—to their color. Skin color, such a powerful piece of the black community experience, had exaggerated meaning in Margaret's family, where her mother "looked like white" and her father, with whom she was so deeply identified, was dark-brown-skinned. Margaret, medium-brown-skinned, was seen by many folks in Vicksburg as "light-skinned," a perception that reflected their mixed response to her "good hair," high intelligence, attractive appearance, and fine family. But with a mother who "looked like white" and a dead brother whose "fair skin and golden curls" were tearfully remembered as Christlike qualities, Margaret never saw herself as "light-skinned."

In a later passage Lightfoot's mother admits: "When I was an adolescent, I thought that it was my father's fault that I was darker." Many Black children come to blame one of their parents for their "bad" features or color. Some Black parents even encourage this; typical of these is the mother who, while applying chemical straighteners to her daughter's tight, kinky hair, would say:

Don't blame me, you got that head of hair from your father. Lord, child, you better not marry no nappy-headed man 'cause I can't deal with no Brillo-headed grandbabies.

Yet even those African-American parents who teach their children that skin color and hair texture are not terribly important must contend with the opinions of strangers. For instance, one Black mother tells of standing in the checkout line at the grocery store with her two daughters, one light skinned with long hair and the other several shades darker, when a woman walked up to the lighter-skinned daughter and sweetly remarked, "Isn't she beautiful?" Fed up with similar scenes, the mother grabbed the two girls and angrily retorted, "Don't you mean, isn't she light?" The woman took offense and backed off, while the mother quickly reassured her daughters that they were equally beautiful.

In other Black families, concerns about skin color do not surface until the children are old enough to date. Then parents and relatives may start to express strong disapproval of darker-skinned boyfriends or girlfriends. A middle-class light-skinned woman named Susie recalls the way her very proper aunt would slip into broken English to caution her about marrying someone "unsuitable," saying, "You don't know nothin' about combin' no nappy hair." In Nettie Jones's novel *The Mischief Makers,* a Black mother expresses a similar concern about her daughter's boyfriend.

His nose had worried her mother more than his beady hair and his chocolate skin. "Makes no sense for you to take us back,'' she'd cried. ''My mama worked too hard to—'' Raphael had run out of the kitchen before she could finish.

Some Black families not only caution their children not to marry someone darker, but insist that the children "lighten the line." A Black professional we'll call David, who is married to a White woman, has five siblings who also married Whites. At the sixth sibling's wedding reception, David's light-skinned father gleefully gave this toast: "Before long, there'll be no more Black left in our family." A dark-skinned woman from Chicago remembers being told to "think about the children" and marry only someone lighter than herself. But she was also told that as a "Black nappy-headed girl" she would probably never get such a man, so she had better get a good education. She is now a Ph.D. and divorced from the light-skinned man she married to please her family.

Black families can also be cruel in their treatment of in-laws who do not measure up on the color barometer. One such case the authors have heard about involves a dark-skinned Black man who married a light-skinned woman from a colorstruck family in Mississippi. The in-laws eventually learned to accept him, but they continued to refuse to allow him in their house on New Year's Day—they adhered to an old superstition that having a dark-skinned Black in one's home on New Year's Day spelled bad luck for the rest of the year.

Not all Black parents want their children to marry someone as light as or lighter than themselves. One dark-skinned professional woman with dreadlocked hair, divorced from a White Englishman, was worried to distraction that her son would marry an Asian woman he had been dating for several years. The mother was determined that he marry someone at least as dark as she was, and she admitted that, if she could, she would arrange his marriage simply to prevent him from marrying someone light.

Pressure from Black parents to "lighten" or "darken" the line can lead some children to rebel. Light-skinned teenagers, in particular, may intentionally date Blacks who are darker. As one prominent African-American businessman recalls:

There was a time in the 60s when I would actively seek out only tar black women to date. No puke yellow black women or snow queens for me. Dark-skinned women were not only a way for me to confirm my blackness but also a way for me to rebel against my parents and their bourgeois ways.

When families are extended through divorce and remarriage, bringing light-skinned and dark-skinned Black children from previous relationships together under one roof, tensions over color differences can become explosive. Color-prejudiced stepparents may reject stepchildren who are too light or too dark. Singer and actress Eartha Kitt, whose stepfather spurned her for being half White, recalls him saying, "I won't have that little yellow gal in my house." Kitt's mother, forced to choose between her daughter and the man she loved, gave the child away, first farming her out to relatives and eventually having her placed in a foster home.

Biracial families also have the potential to produce enormous variations in color and features among their children, and one might expect them to experience intense color conflicts as well. Instead, in interview after interview that we conducted with the adult biracial children of Black-White marriages, all maintained that their parents had been very much attuned to color issues. Perhaps because the parents had thought carefully about the consequences of race mixing, they proved to be better equipped to handle color-related conflicts than many Black parents.

Color preferences all too often come into play when Black families adopt. In the "Black baby market," light-skinned babies go first, a fact that disturbs many Black activists. Zena Olglesby, the founder and executive director of Los Angeles' Institute of Black Parenting, reports that about 40 percent of the Black couples wanting to adopt specifically request children who are light skinned. He tries to combat this syndrome by encouraging prospective parents to look at children of all skin tones, but the practice of choosing children by color is widespread. In 1990, the American Civil Liberties Union filed a report charging the New York City Child Welfare Administration with making foster-home placements on the basis of skin color and hair texture. Evidence from case records indicated that 72 percent of the children available for adoption or foster-home placement were described not just by race but also by color. Sydney Duncan, the president of a child-welfare agency in Detroit called Homes for Black Children, points out, however, that skin-color information is not necessarily discriminatory but helps Black couples adopt children who look something like themselves. Others contend that darker-skinned middle-class Black couples in particular request children with light skin and straight hair. In his book on the Black bourgeoisie, *Certain People,* Stephen Birmingham claims that some wealthy Black couples who are able to have children themselves instead adopt light-skinned children to avoid the possibility of producing a dark-skinned child.

With the advent of reliable birth-control methods and legal abortion, the pool of White babies available for adoption started to shrink during the sixties and seventies. Child welfare champions initially saw this as an opportunity to place needy Black children in the homes of childless White couples, and many adoption agencies modified their policies of matching a baby's racial and physical traits (including skin color, eye color, and hair texture) to those of the prospective parents. But White families who adopted biracial children often did nothing to nurture the Black heritage of their mixed Black-White children. This situation alarmed many members of the National Association of Black Social Workers (NABSW), who asserted that only Black families could give Black children a positive sense of racial identity. In 1972 the NABSW passed a resolution opposing the adoption of Black children, including those who were biracial, by White parents. Critics of this policy point out that White parents are better than no parents and cite research indicating that Black children raised by White parents rarely suffer identity problems. Despite nearly two decades of such criticism, however, the NABSW reaffirmed its opposition to transracial adoptions in 1989. By 1987, thirty-five states had also passed laws prohibiting the adoption of Black children by White families.

Challenges to a biracial child's sense of self often come from outside the home, in the form of taunts from neighborhood children and schoolmates. "Light, bright, and damn near white, your daddy's Black and your mammy's White" is a common playground chant, along with "You're half baked, your momma didn't cook you long enough." Jeering about color appears to be a staple of the Black child's repertoire of insults.

A Black nurse from Knoxville we'll call Marie experienced her near-white skin color as a curse on her childhood. She tried everything to make herself darker, including staying out in the sun all day, so that her schoolmates would stop calling her "school bus," "zebra," "sunshine," and "yellow submarine." (Very dark skinned Blacks are called "shine," "sambo," "aunt Jemima," and "blackie.") The taunts never did stop, nor did Marie's schoolmates stop leaving cans of Mello Yello soda at her seat in the lunchroom. To this day Marie says that she cannot stomach the taste or sight of Mello Yello.

One light-skinned, green-eyed woman remembers that her younger brother was always getting beaten up because of his fair skin color. The other children would yell, "Your momma was messing around with a White man. There's no way you can be yo' daddy's child." And the singer Lena Horne, in her autobiography, recalls that when she moved to Florida as a small girl, the children in her new neighborhood would shout, "Yaller! Yaller! Got a White daddy! Shame! Shame! Shame!"

Superficially, taunts about color may seem the same as calling a child with glasses "four eyes" or a fat child "tubby"—part of the inevitable cruelties of childhood. Yet children can never outgrow skin color as they do other childhood traits, cannot change it by going on a diet or getting contact lenses, and may be less likely to find reassurance at home. While the parents of Black children often prepare them for the possibility that White children may call them "nigger," few parents seem to warn them about hateful name-calling from their "own people." Black parents should teach their children not to tease or judge their peers on the basis of color, emphasizing that skin color has nothing to do with either beauty or Black identity. Parents also need to coach children who are especially light or dark on how to handle taunts about their color or features.

Childhood friends who have quite different skin colors may find it increasingly difficult to maintain their closeness as they become teenagers. Light-skinned adolescents may discover that their popularity is rising and perhaps will conclude that friendships with dark-skinned chums might cost them socially. In no other developmental phase is skin color so closely linked to attractiveness, popularity, and self-worth, especially for Black girls, who throughout junior high and high school learn to compete over looks. As one Black high-school girl puts it:

> The most popular girls in the school are nearly always light-skinned. If a dark-skinned girl is allowed to "hang with them" it is either because she has a car or is from a wealthy family. Otherwise, she isn't going to cut it.

Black teenage boys also have to struggle with the significance of color, but, perhaps because boys are more likely to learn to compete on the playing field and in the classroom, issues of color are not as central to their sense of self-worth. In *A Question of Color,* a public-television documentary about intraracial color discrimination, director Kathe Sandler interviewed two Black male friends, Keyonn and Keith (nicknamed "Shay"), about how skin color affected their relationship.

Keyonn: Shay is always the cute one. He's the cute one cause he's the one with the light skin and the nice hair. And it's like, he smiles and gives everybody that low, adorable look, and it's like, Shay is always the cute one. And that has even gone as far as to the point where I be trying to talk to somebody and they be like, "Yah, you're cute n' all, but . . . but, who's the light-skinned one?" And that's like . . . that's rough!

Shay: He may feel at the time real rejected, just a little rejection. But yet, he and I are above that. We know that I'm light-skinned and he knows that my hair is a better texture, or ya' know, a different texture. It's no better, it's just a different texture . . . and, that being in America, people like white. People like light.

Keyonn: We don't even discuss it between the two of us and we're best friends. I mean, I know why I don't bring it up. I don't bring it up because I wouldn't want to cause an argument over something like that. Cause we're not friends over the color of our skin. We're friends over the people that we are.

Although Keyonn and Shay seem to have a healthy attitude, it took a documentary for them to get their feelings out into the open. Likewise, on *Teen Summit,* a talk show on cable's Black Entertainment Television (BET) channel, a round-table discussion on colorism revealed a complex of emotions. One dark-skinned Black teenager admitted that she resented people telling her, "You're pretty for a dark-skinned girl." A light-skinned girl spoke about her embarrassment over male friends who made fun of dark-skinned girls by saying, "If you put oil on a dark-skinned girl, she'll look like a patent-leather shoe." A teenage boy astutely pointed out that skin-color discrimination within the Black community "is part of a bigger problem that all . . . minorities in a White society [must] deal with."

On college campuses as well as in high schools, Blacks of similar skin color tend to stick together. Very dark skinned Black women often are disappointed to discover that even beyond high school they may still be treated as social outcasts. In *Invisibility Blues: From Pop to Theory,* Michele Wallace writes that even during the radical sixties the darker-skinned sisters at Howard University usually ended up staying in their dorm together on weekend nights.

These misfits, all dark without exception, all with Afros that were too nappy, chose to stay in and watch television or listen to records rather than take advantage of the score of one-night stands they could probably achieve before being taunted into running to their parents as "fallen women." . . . But no one talked about why we stayed in on Friday and Saturday nights on a campus that was well known for its parties and night life. . . . Guzzling gin, cheating at poker, choking on cigarettes that dangled precariously from the corners of our mouths, we'd signify. "If we could only be woman (white) enough" was the general feeling of most of us as we trotted off to bed.

While many college students cling to friends who mirror their own coloring, there are exceptions. For example, a Black woman we'll call Audrey says that among her four best friends in college (three women and a man we'll call Greg) skin color ranged across the spectrum and that as a group they either ignored or joked about their color differences. Still, one of the friends, a brown-skinned woman we'll call Kim, could never join fully in the joking—the subject of color was too emotionally raw for her. Audrey described what happened one day in her dorm room when all five friends were present.

Greg was doing his usual flirting, going around the room saying stuff like, "Come here my spicy cinnamon princess, here is my ebony queen, and this is my vanilla fantasy," but when he got to Kim, she was glaring at him, and so he decided to skip over her. Later, when Kim overheard that Greg had called her a "fat, funky Black bitch," for being so uptight about her color, things were never quite the same again between them.

Color distinctions also characterize certain Black fraternities and sororities (as discussed in Chapter Two) and may subtly influence the selection of beauty queens. Historically, homecoming queens at Black colleges and universities were nearly always light skinned, but now dark-skinned campus queens are becoming the norm. Yet when a Black woman is elected homecoming queen on a predominantly White campus, she is invariably light skinned.

Presumably color is less of an issue in the friendships of those in their twenties and beyond than it is during the cliquish, peer-obsessed years of high school and college. Yet color and features do sometimes influence same-sex relationships among mature adults, especially women. The closest Black women friends are still, more often than not, of similar coloring, perhaps because women prefer friends who are more or less of equal "status" in terms of their attractiveness and desirability to men. Men, however, less invested in their physical appearance, tend to compete over occupational success and money and are likely to form their friendships on that common ground.

Of course, some Black women of radically different skin colors do transcend such concerns. One very light skinned Black nurse in her late twenties who worked at a hospital in upstate New York describes what happened when she was transferred to a new department headed by a dark-skinned female supervisor.

> On the first day of work, I thought to myself, "I better start looking now for a new job because this dark-skinned woman is gonna hate me; they always do." I stuck it out, though, and then one night my boss and I both had to work late. We got to talking and discovered we had something in common— being fed up with the skin color issue. We shared our respective pain about being too dark and too light, and for the first time, we were both able to laugh about all "this color crap." We have been best friends ever since. Still, when we go out together, we often get these weird looks. Strangers even come up to us to ask, "What in the world do you two have in common?"

To their credit, these two women have not let the rudeness of strangers interfere with their friendship. Yet a letter to the "*Ebony* Advisor" from a twenty-seven-year-old light-skinned Black woman tells another story. This woman had gone to a club one evening with a darker-skinned girlfriend and had been approached several times by Black athletes and businessmen, while her friend was approached only once. When she commented on all this attention, the dark-skinned friend said defensively, "The guys were blind to pass over a beautiful cocoa-brown chick for a pale yellow girl." The first woman retorted, among other things, that "Lighter-skinned women were born to dominate chocolate-brown ones" and "The only black men . . . brown women get are the leftovers we don't want." The darker-skinned friend has not spoken to her since, and the woman was writing to ask what she could say to make her dark-skinned friend forgive her. The "*Ebony* Advisor" had this stern reply: "You owe an apology to millions of Black people—including, undoubtedly, many of your own past and present relatives—who happen to be a few shades darker than you are.''

That a difference in skin color could destroy a friendship between two Black women is disturbing, but it is also understandable in a society that is both racist and sexist. Women, regardless of racial background, are judged by how they look, and for Black women good looks are still likely to be defined by the lightness of their skin. Light-skinned Black women are in demand among most Black men, especially men who are darker, because of the possibility they offer of "lightening the line." Add to this the shortage of marriageable Black men, and many Black women feel as if they are competing in a seller's market. The situation divides friends and disrupts families, especially when parents put pressure on their children to marry particular types. Such an erosion of close relationships might be prevented if Black men and women were to explore together the role of color in their lives.

7. Dating and Mating: A Question of Color

Whenever I see a Black man holding hands with a White woman
and he's noticed that I've seen him, he immediately drops her hand.
Is there shame in his game or what?
—TONYA

Go to any Black nightclub and observe how fast men's heads turn when a light-skinned Black woman crosses the room. Yet ask these same men whether color prejudice still affects the Black community, and most would insistently deny that it does. From personal experience, African-American women usually know better; they know that most Black men prefer their women to be "light, bright, and some-times White." Color does matter, and it matters a lot in the realm of dating and mating. Not that African-American women don't have their own color preferences. The pattern is less clearcut, however; as a group, just as many Black women reject Black men for being too light skinned as for being too dark. The Black gay and lesbian community is also affected by traditional color biases, perhaps because regardless of sexual orientation, a light-skinned Black partner, or even a White partner, on one's arm conveys social status. Sadly, it seems the most intimate of relationships are still governed by the politics of color and race.

Sexual attraction usually begins at the level of physical appearance, and every culture prizes certain attributes over others, be they small feet, a slender neck, or a hairy chest. It would seem logical to conclude that skin color preferences operate in the same way, that a Black man who prefers women with light skin and long hair is no different from a White man who prefers women with blond hair and blue eyes. Yet within the African-American community skin color and feature preferences are not just personal; they are political. Blacks often judge each other on the basis of the skin color of those with whom they date and mate. The Black man who goes out exclusively with light-skinned women may be accused of having a color complex. But if he dates only very dark women he risks the accusation that, for whatever reason, he cannot do any "better"; or, if he is light-skinned himself, he may arouse the suspicion that he is just trying to get back to his "roots."

Still, some Blacks claim that color has nothing to do with the way Black men and women pair off. If that were truly so, however, an equal number of dark-skinned and light-skinned women would be married to successful Black men, and, interracially, Black women and White men would marry as often as Black men and White women do. That is not the case. Clear color preferences characterize the romances of African-American men and women, both intraracially and interracially.

In the fifties, the anthropologist Melville Herskovits identified a distinct pattern of successful Black men marrying Black women who were lighter than they. Of the successful Harlem couples he studied, only 29 percent of the wives were darker than their husbands. Of the other couples, 56.5 percent of the wives were lighter than their spouses and 14.5 percent were about the same color.

Fascination with color, particularly with light-skinned women, was supposed to have ended with the sixties, but the preference remains. In a 1980 survey for *Ebony,* Ken and Mamie Clark reported that 30 percent of Black men, as opposed to 15 percent of Black women, specifically desired a light-skinned partner, and in 1985, sociologists Elizabeth Mullins and Paul Sites found that eminent Black men were in fact more likely to have light-skinned spouses than were eminent Black women. Free-lance reporter Marianne Ilaw, a contributing editor of *Chocolate Singles,* also reports that personal ads placed by women who describe themselves as "light-skinned" seem to elicit considerably more responses than other ads. And a review of the personals section reveals a significant number of male requests for women with light skin and/or long hair.

Filmmaker Spike Lee offers a rather blunt explanation of why so many Black men continue to be drawn to lighter-skinned Black women. In an article for *Essence* by Jill Nelson, Lee was quoted as saying:

> Whether black men admit it or not, they feel light-skinned women are more attractive than dark-skinned, and they'd rather see long hair than a short Afro, because that's closer to white women. That comes from being inundated with media from the time you're born that constantly fed you the white woman as the image of beauty. That's both conscious and unconscious. . . . But on the whole, talking to my friends and knowing men, I see that a premium is put on light-skinned sisters with long hair.

Lee touches on the connection between images of power and the attraction to light or white skin. A Black man is aware that the way others judge him often depends on the attractiveness of the woman he is escorting. For the dark-skinned Black man, having a beautiful light-skinned woman at his side instantly communicates to others that he has "made it."

Yet a light-skinned wife is not always an asset for a successful Black man, especially if he is in the public eye. When the dark-skinned Marion Barry first campaigned for mayor of Washington, D.C., as a militant advocate of Black causes, some Blacks accused him of hypocrisy, since he had, after all, married a light-skinned woman. Afraid that his wife, Effi, was becoming a political liability, Barry bought her a sunlamp and told her to try to make herself darker. When that failed, he sent her to the Hilton Head Beach Resort in South Carolina to work on a suntan. Leave it to a politician to understand and manipulate the politics of color!

A Black man who has won the affections of a lighter-skinned woman may sometimes discover that there is a dark side to the relationship. He may start to question whether a beautiful light-skinned woman could ever really love a dark-skinned man like himself. This kind of painful self-doubt is evident in the comments of one dark-skinned man married to a lighter-skinned woman, as quoted in Calvin Hernton's *Sex and Racism in America:*

> I see her sometimes looking at me when I am naked or just milling around the house—I see the resentment in her well-guarded eyes. Whenever I do something she doesn't like, she always calls me a black bastard. If she catches me in a lie, I'm not a lying bastard, I'm a *black* bastard. If I cheat on her, I'm not a cheating bastard, I'm a *black* bastard. No matter what it is she's mad at me about, I'm a black bastard.

Other darker-skinned husbands express their insecurities more violently. One light-skinned woman who was formerly married to a prominent black-skinned businessman from Los Angeles recalls how her ex-husband would parade her in front of others, praising her "fine" bloodline and proudly predicting that their children were going to be "high yella." Yet privately he would punish her for being lighter than he, slapping her around, calling her a "half-breed bitch," and angrily accusing her of thinking she was "too good" for him. She tearfully describes what usually happened after one of their frequent fights.

> He would beat me as we made love. He wanted to hear me whimper. Whimper was all I dare do. Never did I dare cry out. Then after we made love he would turn on the lights and look at my pale, bruised body and smile. Then he would say how beautiful the love marks looked against my "white" skin. Wiping the tears from my eyes, he would proclaim, "You love it when I'm in command, don't you? You're a real woman."

Abuse of a light-skinned woman also occurs in Zora Neale Hurston's novel *Their Eyes Were Watching God.* When the dark-skinned Tea Cake whips his light-skinned girlfriend, Janie, he is able to conquer his fear that he is not good enough for her. Tea Cake discovers that beating Janie garners him respect from other Black men, too, including one named Sop-de-Bottom.

"Tea Cake, you sho is a lucky man," Sop-de-Bottom told him. "Uh person can see every place you hit her. Ah bet she never raised her hand tuh hit yuh back, neither. Take some un dese ol' rusty black women and dey would fight yuh all night long and next day nobody couldn't tell you ever hit 'em. Dat's de reason Ah done quit beatin' mah woman. You can't make no mark on 'em at all. Lawd! wouldn't Ah love tuh whip un tender woman lak Janie! Ah bet she don't even holler. She jus' cries, eh Tea Cake?"

At the end of the novel, Janie kills Tea Cake in self-defense; in an *Essence* essay entitled "Embracing the Dark and the Light," novelist Alice Walker speculates that Hurston was attempting to expose the myth that light-skinned Black women are more fragile and more readily subdued than those who are darker skinned. Walker also comments that any light-skinned Black woman who sells herself as a prize to a successful dark-skinned Black man is "more to be pitied than blamed."

Beautiful light-skinned women are sometimes called "Black American princesses" and assumed to have a superiority complex. Yet while some light-skinned women are raised to think that they are better than others and do develop an "attitude," many others resent the stereotype and simply want to be accepted for who they are—not seen as trophies by Black men. One highly attractive light-skinned Black model named Shannon has said:

When I go to clubs, Black men won't even ask me to dance. I have to ask them. Most Black men make assumptions about me based on my looks and my color. And when someone does ask me out and I happen to say no, then they accuse me of liking White men. But I have never liked White men.

Of course, there are some Black men who marry lighter-skinned women for reasons unrelated to color. A successful Black engineer with a beautiful light-skinned Black wife defended his relationship by saying, "Not all Black men who have a light-skinned woman or wife purposely chose her for that reason. It may just be that they've found the woman they love and that she simply happens to be light skinned."

Do Black men ever prefer light-skinned women as substitutes for the White women they really desire? A phrase Black men sometimes use to describe a light-skinned Black woman is "She's light but not quite"—meaning not quite White. This connection between light skin and white skin is an old one, dating back to the last century. It was even celebrated by a "Negro punster" in this song:

> *She got to be white, Jack—*
> *'Cause white is right*
> *Both day and night!*
> *She got to be old and white,*
> *'Cause if she's old*
> *She's been white longer!*
> *She got to be big and white,*
> *'Cause if she's big*
> *She's much more white!*
> *But listen, Jack—*
> *If she just can't be white*
> *Then let her be real light brown!*

Before the sixties few Black men risked dating or mating with White women. In some parts of the country they could still be lynched for doing so. But during that rebellious decade social mores loosened, and Black men and White women began to come together with greater frequency. The Black historian Paula Giddings believes that this pattern of interracial romance began when liberal northern White women went south to work in the civil rights movement. Some southern Black men, eager to "affirm their manhood" by having sex with White women, expressed interest in these northern women, and many of the women responded with enthusiasm. Although these extracurricular activities met the needs of both Black men and White women, they frustrated a number of Black women. Tensions grew in the civil rights camps, and some of the White women were even asked to leave. But the racial barrier had fallen.

Various other explanations have been offered for the attraction between Black men and White women. One theory holds that the fact that White women were historically forbidden to Black men made them that much more desirable. It was a "power trip" for a Black man finally to possess this ideal beauty; at last the shoe was on the other foot—he was now the master and she the slave.

Similarly, William Grier and Price Cobbs have proposed, in *Black Rage,* that the Black man's desire is rooted in rage stemming from his unconscious desire to seek revenge for his slave past.

> In possessing the white woman [the black man] sees himself as degrading her (a function of his own feelings of degradation), in this instance sharing the community's feeling that a white woman who submits to a black lover becomes as debased as he. In this way he may feel the gratification of turning the tables on his white oppressor and thus becoming the instrument through which a white person is degraded.

A Black Harvard sociology professor, Charles Willie, himself married to a White woman, attributes the attraction to a couple's separate but comparable vulnerabilities—he in being a Black male, she in being female. The equality in the relationship, and the uncertainty of dominance, generates sexual tension.

A Black filmmaker from Chicago offers another view.

> White women have always been off-limits to black men. The closest some black men could get to a white woman was through girlie magazines. So over the years a group of black boys grew up masturbating with the white girls in *Penthouse.* Because that's all they saw. This caused them to go out and date any 250-pound greasy white woman they could find, whose only redeeming quality was that they had blond hair, blue eyes, and white skin.

Obviously, not all Black men are attracted to women who are White or are lighter than themselves. In fact, research by Robert L. Douglas, an associate professor and chair of the Pan-African Studies Department at the University of Louisville, indicates that the more strongly a man identifies with his African heritage, the less likely he is to be attracted to light-skinned Black women. There are also Black men who seek out dark-skinned women to communicate unequivocally to others their "pro-Black" stance or to rebel against parents who are colorstruck. Some Black men pursue dark-skinned women because they find them less "stuck on themselves" and more responsive, especially if they have been rejected by men who thought them too dark. Some men who are themselves light skinned marry dark-skinned women in the hope that their children will look unmistakably Black. A light-skinned New York journalist, Michel Marriott, remembers how he felt when he learned that his partner, a dark-skinned Zimbabwean from southern Africa, was pregnant. In an article for *Essence* he wrote:

> At the time I jested with friends that I was repairing the violence done to my genetic pool by returning to the original stock . . . At least my sperm was going back to Africa.

Other light-skinned men capitalize on their color advantage in seeking a mate, using their color as a commodity to be exchanged in the interpersonal marketplace. Such a strategy is evident in the following personal ads, in which color gets top billing (emphasis ours).

> **BABY FACE. Light-skinned** black male, 31, 165 lbs. You're a woman 21–30 who loves Great America, vegetarian dining, physical fitness and dancing, look no further. No smoking or drugs please. . . .

> **SINGLE BLACK MALE, 5'11", light complexion,** very attractive, likes modern rock, dance music, etc. Free spirited

and adventurous. Seeking attractive white, Asian or Hispanic female 21–35, who's fun to be with and looks good in black. . . .

Plenty of Black women respond to these kinds of ads with color prejudices of their own. Dark-skinned women, in particular, may aggressively pursue Black men who are lighter, leaving some of the men to wonder if the women just want to dip into their pools of pale genes. Although the desire for lighter-skinned children is indeed a motivation for some women, basic sexual attraction is another. One college student has said that she would never date a dark-skinned Black man because she was turned off by the contrast of "pink lips on black skin." A waitress has professed to a strong dislike of light-skinned Black men because, in her opinion, they lacked certain "soul brother" credentials. As one dark-skinned professional woman has said, "When I see these Africanized Black brothers looking the way my ancestors may have looked, I get turned on." And another Black woman, a secretary, says that the darker the man's skin, the less inhibited and more animalistic, exotically erotic, and masculine she found him to be—the same justification some White women offer for their "jungle fever."

Some African Americans, male and female, simply gravitate toward those with approximately the same skin color as themselves. Different patterns are associated with the various skin-color groupings. Blacks in the medium-brown range are typically the least concerned with color and may prefer partners who are equally unconcerned. Those Blacks with very light skin who go out only with other very light-skinned Blacks are often deracinated. They may come from haut-bourgeois families in which dating and mating choices are made with an eye to social status and the prospect of light-skinned children. Blacks who are very dark skinned and date only other dark-skinned Blacks may also be making a statement about their social or economic status. If both persons are financially secure, the dark color preference may reflect the freedom to make a conscious and personal choice. But if both are very poor, it may simply mean that their choice of partners is limited to their own socioeconomic class, in which most people are dark-skinned. This is particularly true for the impoverished dark-skinned man. Poor women who are light skinned have the best chance of trading in on their color to flee the "hood," leaving the predominantly darker-skinned women behind.

A growing number of Blacks are venturing to marry across the racial barrier. In 1970, only 1.5 out of every 1,000 marriages in the United States, or a total of 65,000, were between Blacks and Whites; by 1990, the figure was 4 out of every 1,000 marriages, or a total of 218,000 (71 percent of them between Black men and White women, only 29 percent between Black women and White men). Interracial marriage is much more socially acceptable than it was in 1958, when a White man named Richard Loving was arrested when he brought back to his hometown in Virginia a Black woman named Mildred Jeter whom he had married in Washington, D.C. Accused of violating the state's antimiscegenation laws, Loving faced a prison sentence of up to five years. The sentence was later suspended on the condition that he and his wife not set foot in Virginia for the next twenty-five years. Since the Lovings did not feel that they had done anything criminally wrong, they sued. The case went all the way to the U.S. Supreme Court, and in 1967 the court's decision in *Loving* v. *Virginia* overturned the existing antimiscegenation laws in Virginia and in fifteen other states.

More recently, surveys conducted by the National Opinion Research Center of the University of Chicago have indicated that tolerance for interracial relationships is increasing. In 1972, 39 percent of Whites said that interracial marriages should be illegal; by 1991, the number had dropped to 17 percent. Acceptance of interracial marriage is even higher among Blacks. In 1980, 20 percent of Blacks thought that interracial marriages should be banned; by 1991, the figure had dropped to a low of 7 percent.

These figures may sound encouraging, but they do not necessarily translate into actual support for interracial relationships. In an ideal world, interracial liaisons would elicit only indifference, but most Americans, Black or White, fail the "no-blink test" when they encounter an interracial couple on the street. And sometimes interracial couples, who are derisively called "zebras," do more than aston-ish—they enrage.

Blacks who cross the race line are often accused by other Blacks of selling out. The charge is most often brought against an African American who takes a White spouse after garnering some degree of power or social success. A surprising number of Black leaders and entertainers have historically had White husbands or wives, and the trend continues today. The early abolitionist, writer, and orator Fred-erick Douglass divorced his first wife, Annie Murray Douglass, a dark-skinned Black woman (who allegedly made the sailor suit Doug-lass wore when he escaped from slavery), to marry a White woman. The wives of two former presidents of the NAACP, Walter White and Leslie Perry, were White, and so were the wives of Richard Wright, the author of *Native Son,* and the Black Renaissance painter Archibald Motley. Alex Haley, author of *Roots,* married a White woman, as did Shelby Steele, author of *The Content of Their Char-acter,* the composer and record producer Quincy Jones, playwright August Wilson, actors Sidney Poitier and James Earl Jones, the ath-lete O. J. Simpson, and Supreme Court Justice Clarence Thomas. Shari Belafonte and Whoopi Goldberg were formerly married to Whites, and Diahann Carroll (Vic Damone), Diana Ross (Arne Ness), Leslie Uggams (Graham Pratt), and model Iman (David Bowie) are other celebrities who have had White husbands.

Although not every African American of high social standing "marries out," enough have done so to inspire a variety of theories about the reason. One hypothesis is that Blacks still perceive Whites as superior and marry them to elevate their own status or as proof of their success. Another theory holds that powerful people are simply attracted to each other and that high-profile Blacks have few oppor-tunities to marry other high-status Blacks. Whatever the reason, the marital selections of prominent Blacks are viewed politically, provok-ing concern that these role models may be sending the wrong mes-sage to the Black community when they choose to marry Whites.

Celebrities aside, Beth Austin, who writes regularly for the *Chi-cago Tribune,* has attempted to explain why Blacks and Whites marry, and not all the reasons she cites are negative.

Some people marry out to make the statement that where they've come from is not where they're going. They're saying they were never comfortable in their old lives, and they want something new and different for themselves and their families. By marrying out, they are really marrying into something they've always yearned for. . . . Some people marry out to tell the world that they are rebels . . . and have no interest in a conventional, no-risk marriage [and] . . . some people marry out because they've found someone whose exterior differences are far outweighed by inner qualities that make them feel truly at home.

While the percentage of Black women who marry White men remains small, it is on the rise. In 1980 there were only 45,000 Black women married to White men; by 1987 this number had risen to 56,000 and by 1990 to 61,190. Since the days of slavery, White men have experimented sexually with Black women, but not until recently did many take them as wives.

Again, different reasons are given for this trend. In an article in the conservative *National Review,* D. Keith Mano has speculated that the "female-lib" movement may have alienated White men from White women. "The two groups that drew closest together both financially and temperamentally were black women and white men," Mano wrote, suggesting that traditional values governing husband-wife relationships outweigh cultural differences. While White women tend to disagree with Mano's analysis, some African-American women also believe that the feminist movement is partly responsible for the recent increase in marriages between Black females and White males.

On the other hand, at least one professional Black female prefers White men, especially middle-class professionals, because she finds them more secure and therefore less intimidated by her power, aggressiveness, and self-assurance. Furthermore, she claims that most professional Black men are "egotistical workhorses" who tend to exploit the imbalance in the ratio between marriageable Black men and Black women.

One reason for the rise in the number of Black women willing to date or marry White men is the shortage of eligible Black males. Black women, even those who are light-skinned, are finding it increasingly difficult to find good matches. In some urban areas there are as many as eight marriageable Black women for every marriageable Black man, and during the past twenty years the incidence of Black marriages has dropped by 20 percent. Contributing factors include the high unemployment rate of Black males, even among the college educated; the fact that one in four Black males between the ages of twenty and twenty-nine is in prison (usually serving a longer sentence than a White man convicted for the same crime); and Black-on-Black violence, which has reduced the number of Black men in the inner city and has shortened the average life expectancy of Black men as a whole.

An interracial match is clearly not the answer for every African-American woman looking for a husband. For some the cultural differences are too problematic. Others find that Black features which feel comfortable and right in the presence of other Blacks become mortifying in the presence of Whites. One Black woman became obsessed with the idea that her pubic hair was too "bristly," and she began shaving herself every day so that she wouldn't "scratch" her White lover. Another woman straightened the "edges" of her hair daily so that her "naps" would not show. One extremely white skinned Black woman with gray eyes and high cheekbones had plastic surgery on her nose, the only feature that could have indicated to the White men she was interested in that she was Black. Yet another Black woman washed, blow-dried, straightened, and curled her hair until it fell out—all because she was too embarrassed to wear rollers at night, knowing that her boyfriend's former White girlfriends had "simply flipped their hair into place" every morning.

Yet some White men are drawn to women with undeniably black skin and Africanized features, finding them exotically different. Of course, others limit themselves to Black women with light skin and long hair, perhaps because they are more comfortable with looks that are relatively familiar. And some White men admit that it is a struggle to accept a lover's Blackness. In an article in *Essence* entitled "Guess Who's Coming to Dinner Now?" by Dorothy Tucker, the feelings of a White politician from Detroit about being in an interracial relationship were described this way:

> I seldom think of my girlfriend, Kathy, as black as long as we are out at a restaurant, a cocktail party or playing tennis. [But] I remember once when we woke up in the morning I was staring at her and she looked awfully Black right then. A lot of times I look at her and it's as if she is white; there's no real difference. But every now and then, it depends on what she is wearing and what we're doing, she looks very ethnic and very Black. It bothers me. I don't like it. I prefer it when she's a regular, normal, everyday kind of person.

In some cases, though, a White man pursues a Black woman to satisfy a psychological urge. One handsome White man, the manager of a famous rock band, claims that he likes Black women because of their warmth and kind, motherly ways. It happens that he grew up in a wealthy White racist household and was raised by a Black nanny. He has memories of being rocked to sleep in this woman's arms. As he grew older and heard his parents spout racist ideology, he became confused. How could they despise Black people when it was a Black woman who had first offered him love? Much to his family's dismay, he took to dating Black women, a phenomenon the African-American community calls the "Black-nanny syndrome."

How do Black men feel when they see some of the most desirable Black women with White men? Understandably, some are outraged, and some are concerned about the effect that unchecked intermarriage will have on the future of their race. Others claim that White men do not really love Black women but just have "jungle fever." Some Black men accuse Black women who date Whites of being "gold diggers," and most find it hard to believe that a Black woman could ever forget the years of rape and humiliation that White men inflicted on her female ancestors. In their defense, Black women say that they have not forgotten their legacy of exploitation, but, as one Black woman who is currently dating a White man puts it, "Why should we deprive ourselves of each other because of the history that neither one of us had anything to do with?"

Black women, too, sometimes react with anger and disbelief when they see "their men" with White women. Most assume that a Black man's involvement with a White woman has to do with her color and status, not with love, common interests, or respect. Black women have also observed that Black men rarely seem proud of their interracial dating and often appear embarrassed when Black women see them with White dates. As Tonya, the Black college student quoted at the beginning of the chapter, asked, "Is there shame in his game or what?"

Some White women who date Black men are sensitive to Black women's anger and concern about the shortage of Black men. But they have their own reasons for falling in love with Black men. A middle-aged woman named Nan, blond and blue eyed, who has been dating a dark-skinned Black man for over three years, told the authors:

> If he was the same man—tall and heavy, sorta clumsy—but White, I don't think I'd be attracted to him. There is something about his Blackness, his mannerisms, and his intelligence that I like very much. But I did not specifically go looking for a Black man—it just sort of happened.

Nan added that White men have often found it difficult to believe that there could be any real common interests between her and her Black lover. One White man came up to her in a bar and said, "Tell me the truth, it's the dick, isn't it?" Despite this kind of hostility, interracial dating is likely to increase as more and more Blacks and Whites spend time together at school and at work.

In the Black gay and lesbian community, complexes about color also affect the way couples pair off. A light-skinned Black gay professional said:

> There are basically three types of people who signal their attraction to me: straight [Black] women who don't know I'm

gay, Black men, and White men. With the women, I often feel the main reason they want to go out with me is because I'm light, but with the Black men I have never really felt that my coloring was that much of a factor. As for the White men I've dated, my color is important only to the extent that it is part of a larger package that makes me safe for them—I'm educated, with a prestigious job, and I happen to be a Black with fairly light color. Of course, there are some White men who date Blacks like me because they are dinge queens [White men who date Black men because of the eroticism of black on white skin].

A very dark skinned Black gay actor named Michael, who has been accused of being a "snow queen" (a Black man who "gets off" being with someone White), denies the charge, and insists that his attraction to White men has more to do with class than color. To his chagrin, he claims that he has been unable to find another gay Black man in his own socioeconomic class. Yet he adds, "It makes all the difference in the world to walk into a restaurant with a White man, as opposed to another Black man. We are treated much better because they assume we have money."

Another Black gay actor, Eric F., who has a White boyfriend and is very light skinned, recalls that in high school he was constantly teased not only about his light skin tone but also about his proper speech and his popularity with girls. "Being harassed by my own people" about his color added to Eric's feelings of isolation when he began to explore his own sexuality. He is disturbed by the constant references to color he encounters in the Black gay community. Once he remarked to a dark-skinned Black gay friend that he did not think he was good looking enough to go to bars; the friend replied, "Oh, you would do fine. Guys like nice-looking light-skinned men like you." Eric believes that the same color issues that affect the straight community affect the gay community as well. "All this dinge queen and snow queen stuff is a bunch of crap, and only perpetuates racism in the homosexual community," he says.

Skin color affects Black lesbian relationships, too. As one woman succinctly puts it, "There are as many lesbians as 'breeders' who are colorstruck." Another Black lesbian, Mary Morten, the former president of the Chicago chapter of the National Organization for Women, says that both White and light-skinned Black lesbians sometimes assign special erotic value to dark-skinned Black women, whom they call "African goddesses." Still, such women do not necessarily feel any better about their dark color. Morten had one dark-skinned lesbian friend who, even on vacation, avoided going out in the sunshine because "she didn't want to get any darker than she already was." Morten also recalls the time that a Black woman she did not know called her on the telephone and began describing herself as a "green-eyed, light-skinned stud who was so light she could pass"—as if that was supposed to impress Morten. It did not. "A lot of work still needs to be done in terms of making women feel it doesn't matter what color skin they have," she concludes.

We agree, and we would add that for both sexes and races, more substantive attributes than skin color should go into deciding whom to date and with whom to share one's life.

8. Color Harassment in the Workplace

"You ain't about nothing, girl. You think you're so bad. You need some sun.
Life's been too easy for you. You're gonna have to work for your position here."
—From Tracy Morrow's testimony,
January 1990

Tracy Morrow Walker drove from Seattle across the country to Atlanta because she had heard that there were more government jobs in the South. She had a high-school education and a GS-3 civil-service ranking, and she was soon hired at the Atlanta office of the Internal Revenue Service. Within a few months her white female supervisor had written a favorable job evaluation, and she decided to send for her four-year-old daughter, whom she had left in Seattle. She finally felt secure enough to handle the additional responsibilities of being a single mother.

Not long after her daughter's arrival Walker's luck began to turn. Her first supervisor was promoted and was replaced by a dark-skinned Black woman named Ruby Lewis, from New Orleans. Walker was initially encouraged to see someone of her own race as her supervisor, but it soon became apparent that the new supervisor had taken an immediate and strong dislike to Walker. Whenever Walker, who was several shades lighter, asked Lewis for assistance, Lewis would take the opportunity to put her down. Walker remembered being summoned to the supervisor's office one day and having Lewis shout at her, behind closed doors, "You need to go back where you came from. You need some sun. Why don't you go to Shoney's [a chain of fast-food restaurants in the South] and get a job?" Finally Walker was moved to a corner desk, so close to a filing cabinet that whenever someone wanted to open a drawer she had to get up and move. And although her new desk had no phone on it, Walker was expected to answer the phone on someone else's desk within three rings. Her morale plummeted and her anger grew, especially when she noticed Lewis's generous compliments to the dark-skinned women in the office, including the one now occupying Walker's old desk.

She decided to discuss the rapidly deteriorating situation with Lewis's boss, who sent them both to an employee assistance counselor. The fact that Walker had talked to Lewis's boss only made Lewis madder. Walker then discovered that Lewis was keeping a diary about her. At her rope's end, she went to the Equal Employment Opportunity Commission (EEOC) office and filed a complaint of color discrimination under Title VII of the 1964 Civil Rights Act. A few days later she was fired—only four months after Lewis's arrival in the office.

Attitudes about skin color among African Americans occasionally erupt in this manner in the workplace. Feelings of resentment toward those who are lighter or prejudice against those who are darker are common sources of job-related color harassment. Tensions between Blacks about skin color and features may also be fueled by the tendency of Whites to hire and promote light-skinned Blacks over those who are darker. In the past most African Americans suffering from this kind of color discrimination simply tolerated the abuse. While a few lodged complaints (to no avail) before state human-rights commissions, Tracy Morrow Walker was the first to file charges of color discrimination at the federal level.

Charles A. Moye, Jr., the U.S district judge assigned to the Tracy Morrow case (Walker had meanwhile been divorced and reclaimed her maiden name), reviewed the allegations of color discrimination and decided to hear the case, in part because the wording of Title VII specifically identifies "color" as separate from race, religion, sex, and national origin. Ronald Hall and Midge Wilson were both hired by the plaintiff to serve as expert witnesses in the precedent-setting case. At the center of the opposing trial arguments was the question of whether it was the dark-skinned Lewis or the lighter-toned Morrow who had the color complex. Ron's testimony emphasized that Ruby Lewis was from New Orleans, where there are deep-rooted attitudes about skin color, and that therefore she was prone to react negatively toward a lighter-skinned Black subordinate. Midge, concurring, cited clinical and experimental research indicating that dark-skinned Blacks, especially women, frequently suffered from color discrimination and consequently resented Blacks who were lighter. She testified that a dark-skinned person who comes into a position of authority may be motivated to punish lighter-skinned employees if he or she believes that they have enjoyed unfair advantages because of their lighter color.

Lewis's defense centered on Morrow's work attitude; her attorney claimed that Morrow had been fired for incompetence, not because of her color. After months of deliberation Judge Moye ruled in favor of the IRS and against Tracy Morrow. The charges had been poorly documented, and no witnesses had been found to verify Morrow's claims of color harassment. Nonetheless, Moye conceded that skin-color prejudice between Black coworkers can and often does exist, but he felt that another case might provide a better test of the issue. Morrow's case is now on appeal.

Regardless of the eventual outcome of her case, Tracy Morrow has played an important role in increasing the awareness of Black-on-Black color discrimination in the workplace. At the time of the trial, talk-show hosts and news stations, from Geraldo to CNN, ran features discussing "the last taboo" of the Black community. Some African Americans were embarrassed and angry that their "dirty laundry" was being aired in public, and a few accused Morrow of fabricating the whole story just for the publicity.

If, as Morrow testified, Lewis had indeed said to her, "Life's been too easy for you," Lewis was echoing a sentiment that had its origins in slavery. Before the Civil War, dark-skinned slaves watched from the fields as their owners repeatedly picked mulattoes for the coveted indoor assignments. Masters tended to select lighter-skinned slaves for this more responsible work because they believed that an infusion of White blood helped overcome Negroes' basic inferiority. No scientific proof has ever existed that people of mixed White and Black ancestry were more capable or intelligent than those who were pure Black, but the slave owners believed this was so. The "mulatto hypothesis" served to explain to them why certain Negroes, mostly educated mulattoes, could excel in science and literature when Negroes as a race were supposed to be ineducable.

As long as Whites controlled the job market, the darker one's skin, the darker were one's chances of being hired. Throughout Reconstruction and well into the twentieth century, light-skinned Blacks were hired ahead of equally qualified darker-skinned Blacks, especially for coveted service jobs. Whites derisively called service positions "nigger work," but opportunities for good employment for Blacks were limited, and highly educated mulattoes often worked as porters, waiters, domestic servants, gardeners, and drivers. Because of the restricted job market, mulattoes rarely passed judgment on the basis for their hiring, although they themselves frequently judged others on color and breeding.

A significant number of light-skinned Blacks worked as professionals, though. In the 1930s, Caroline B. Day surveyed more than 800 mulattoes and found that an impressive 44 percent were employed in some professional capacity, with about one-third enjoying solidly middle-class incomes. In a 1982 article in *Essence*, free-lance writer Bonnie Allen observed that "up until World War II—when blacks became a force in the job market . . .—it was easier to get a job if you were lighter skinned simply because you'd had more opportunities for education, and whites felt more secure in your ability to act like a proper Negro."

The passage of the 1964 Civil Rights Act did much to open the job market for Blacks. As White employers scrambled to meet new employment guidelines, some discovered that by employing only light-skinned Blacks they could be in compliance with affirmative-action policies while minimizing the visible presence of new Black employees. Ironically, it was primarily light-skinned Blacks, especially those light enough to pass, who benefited from the antidiscrimination legislation. When Black leaders realized what was happening, they protested, and the practice of hiring "too-white Negroes" subsided. One Chicago government official maintains, however, that to this day a disproportionate number of very light skinned Negroes can be found in civil-service positions. In his opinion, light-skinned Blacks have a better chance not only of being hired but also of being promoted, because "a Negro with light skin will fit better into an office. He won't be so different. The department heads lean toward this type of person." The mulatto hypothesis lives on, and so does the resentment felt by dark-skinned Blacks.

Light-skinned Blacks, acutely aware of their skin-color privilege, usually try to be sensitive about the issue in their relations with darker-skinned coworkers. However, recent changes in the nature of the work force have inadvertently created new tensions. Following the sixties, when educated light-skinned Blacks entered business and the professions in increasing numbers, the kinds of service jobs they would have held in the fifties began to be filled by less-educated, often darker-skinned Blacks. In Illinois, a dark-skinned Black train porter who wore his hair in dreadlocks claimed that he was constantly harassed by an older, lighter-skinned porter. Although his case was dismissed for lack of evidence, it is easy to imagine similar conflicts based on both generational and color differences arising between two Blacks.

According to an article in the *Atlantic Journal Constitution,* a Black female secretary at the Morehouse School of Medicine named Nimat A. Rashid claimed to have been harassed by a lighter-skinned Black supervisor because of her color. In 1990, Rashid filed a complaint of discrimination with the EEOC, the first such case since Tracy Morrow's. Her affidavit stated that Janet Allen, her supervisor, was "prejudiced against attractive, dark-skinned/brown-skinned African-American women" and that as a result Rashid received an unusually heavy workload. The situation allegedly became so difficult that Rashid was forced to resign.

Sometimes a conflict between Black employees begins over something unrelated to skin color, but as tensions grow turns into one of color harassment. Blacks often feel that they should stick together and avoid interpersonal conflict in the office or workplace, but this is an unrealistic goal. When a White male employee has problems with his White supervisor, he will conclude that his boss is abusing him or—giving the boss the benefit of the doubt—that they have a basic personality conflict. If a Black male has the same problems with a White supervisor, he might conclude that his boss is abusive *and* a racist. Similarly, if a White female is having trouble with a male boss, she might think him a sexist. But when a Black man or woman has problems with a Black supervisor, particularly one of the same sex, the employee may feel betrayed and will tend to blame the most visible and sensitive difference between them: any variation in skin color.

A case in point involves two Black men, one light skinned and one darker, who worked for a Black supervisor at the Benton Harbor, Michigan, Public Works Department. Although both men agreed that the boss was an unreasonable man, the lighter-skinned employee thought that the supervisor was slightly nicer to the darker-skinned men in the department, while the darker-skinned man thought that the supervisor treated lighter-skinned men marginally better. Both men were puzzled and angry that a Black man could treat other Blacks so poorly. The lighter-skinned man even accused the residents of Benton Harbor, 90 percent of whom are Black, of suffering from a "plantation mentality," citing a recent mayoral election in which a Black candidate beat a White candidate by only fifty-four votes.

Tensions based on color harassment can also develop between Blacks working at the same level. One light-skinned Black woman, employed at IBM in Chicago, said that one or two of her Black co-workers (perhaps jealous of her good relationship with their White boss) frequently called her, among other things, a "high yella bitch." Because the coworkers knew this upset her, they kept it up. Another Black woman reports that while she was letting her dreadlocks grow out, her Black colleagues harassed her unmercifully about her "nappy-looking" hair. Such intraracial discrimination is difficult for African Americans to resolve, in part because so many of them work for White supervisors. They fear, perhaps rightly, that a White boss will not understand the problem and later might use the information against a Black employee.

While affirmative action has helped thousands of Blacks get jobs, programs based on preferential treatment can create conflicts for lighter-skinned Blacks, especially those light enough to pass. One Black woman from Chicago who has near-white skin and blue eyes says that she refused to take advantage of minority scholarships because she did not want anyone, Black or White, to think she was taking unfair advantage of funds targeted for "others." Although proud of her Black heritage, she also tries to downplay any mention of race during job interviews for fear that a potential employer will think she is using her minority status to influence the hiring decision.

In Denver, one very light skinned Black woman was accused of using her race in order to secure a teaching contract with the Denver Public Schools. This woman, Mary Walker, is light eyed and fair skinned with an unusual family history. Her parents were very light skinned Blacks who decided for economic and survival reasons to raise their fourteen children as White (one child died in infancy). Although skin color and features varied somewhat within the family, all but one of the children were designated as "White" on their birth certificates. When Mary was old enough to understand the family secret, she was told, as were her other siblings, that she could be "Black" at home but that at school and elsewhere, she had to be "White." Admonitions about not listening to soul music and the necessity of straightening her hair were a constant part of Walker's upbringing. She went along with the double identity until she went away to college in the sixties and discovered that she wanted to explore her Blackness. Yet when she tried to join the Black student union she was rejected for being too White.

In the years that followed, Walker earned a master's degree in education, gave birth to a child, developed a kidney disease that required ten years of dialysis, and eventually underwent a kidney transplant operation. Two years following her operation, Walker was working as a substitute teacher in the Denver Public School system and continuing to apply for a job as a full-time contract teacher. Questions were raised about her health, but after two years as a substitute teacher, she was finally awarded a nonrenewable contract to teach for five months at an inner city school. There Mary campaigned hard for improvements in Black children's education. She particularly championed the hiring of Black teachers as there were none at this particular school. Her Black students blossomed under her tutelage.

To her great disappointment, however, Mary's contract was not renewed for the next year. At the time, she was in the process of suing the Denver school system for discrimination based on her medical history, and during the course of this ongoing lawsuit, the issue of her race surfaced. The Denver Public School System noticed a discrepancy between the race indicated on her birth certificate and the fact that she had checked Black as well as White on her job application. One school administrator demanded to know why a White woman cared so much about Black children, and the head of school personnel even stated that Mary had changed her race from White to Black so that she would have a better chance of being hired in that particular district. Amid the controversy, the Office of Civil Rights ruled against her, and closed the case. The Walker case, however, continues in the federal district court.

Mary Walker's complicated story illustrates that Blacks who are light enough to pass can be accused of trying to use their race to gain an occupational advantage. Many Black employees find themselves in a double bind about how best to express their race and identity at work. If they know that they have been hired because a corporation needs more Blacks, they feel guilty and confused. They may wonder whether their White coworkers think that their race has earned them preferential treatment. If they are light skinned, they may also wonder whether darker-skinned Blacks were passed over for the job. Some try to avoid the issue of race altogether by blending in quietly. However, if they never speak up about racial issues other Blacks may label them "oreos," and they will have forfeited the opportunity to try to bring about changes in the workplace.

As Blacks in a predominantly White working environment attempt to strike a balance between strongly identifying as Black and quietly assimilating as White, the issue may be further complicated by class considerations. Blacks who are dark skinned *and* middle-class are sensitive to the fact that their dark skin may lead others to think that they are lower-class. To avoid such a judgment, they may pay close attention to their wardrobes, their manners, and particularly their language. Middle-class Blacks who are light skinned are usually not as self-conscious about their Blackness. They may feel more comfortable discussing issues of race or using Black "jive" while joking around.

White supervisors are generally unaware of these nuances. In their ignorance, they may unintentionally create color-related conflicts among Black employees, especially by primarily hiring and promoting Blacks with light skin. Such tendencies exist even within the Black community. For example, a disproportionate number of Black women working at many Black corporations are light skinned. Writer Bonnie Allen believes that the hiring and promoting of light-skinned female employees "reflects the sexual preferences of the men in charge." Obviously, this kind of colorism hurts the chances of dark-skinned Black women who are trying to get ahead in the business world.

Corporate policies dictating appearance and dress codes may also discriminate against Black female employees. Roughly half of all women, Black as well as White, are clustered in a narrow range of low-paying "pink-collar" jobs: secretary, receptionist, salesperson, ticketing agent. The men who typically do the hiring still consider "looking good" a prerequisite for such jobs. Many businesses have strict rules about makeup and hair, and some corporations, including the major airlines, specifically prohibit employees in particular jobs from wearing certain Black hairstyles. A Black flight attendant with one of the major carriers says that she was permitted to wear cornrow braids on regular domestic flights but that her hairstyle disqualified her from working military charters. There seemed to be no logical reason for the rule, but it could not be broken. Such regulations make life difficult for a woman with nappy hair. Cheryl Tatum, a food and beverage cashier at the Hyatt Regency Hotel outside of Washington, D.C., went to work one day with her hair in neat, professionally styled cornrows. She was immediately pulled aside by her White supervisor and informed that her hair was not right for the Hyatt code of appearance. Tatum continued to wear the cornrows—the style was very expensive and was meant to last four weeks—and despite satisfactory performance ratings she was dismissed. She thought this was grossly unfair and filed a complaint of discrimination against the corporation under Title VII of the 1964 Civil Rights Act. After years of negotiation, Hyatt finally settled out of court, but the experience left Tatum bitter. She has since become self-employed and doubts that she will ever enter a White-dominated work setting again.

It is hard to say whether such treatment of Black women in the workplace is more sexist or more racist. Many working Black women, already burdened by shopping, child care, and housework, must spend yet more of their energy in hair grooming. What precious little extra time and money they have is consumed by frequent trips to the beauty salon for styling or straightening. And the ritual never ends: switching to an unprocessed style, like a short natural or cornrows, is not an option in many workplaces.

Some Black men suffer from a unique form of work-related discrimination associated with the texture of their hair. Pseudofolliculitis (PFD) is a skin disorder in which the closely cut ends of coarse beard hairs curve back and re-enter the skin, making daily shaving a painful ordeal. The condition affects mostly Black men, and wearing a beard offers an easy solution to the problem. But, once again, many companies have appearance codes that dictate a clean-shaven look. Afflicted Black men have the choice of suffering quietly, quitting the job and finding another that does not require daily shaving, or filing a lawsuit against an employer who rigidly enforces a ''no beard'' policy. In 1990, one PFD victim did successfully fight and win a case against Domino's Pizza after he was fired for not shaving. Another Black man, Donald Boyd, won a similar case in 1983 against the University of Maryland security department; he had been fired after he abandoned his ten-year struggle with PFD to grow a quarter-inch beard. Perhaps if a larger percentage of Whites had PFD, employers would allow exceptions to their ''no beard'' policies.

In some cases, racism at a high level of management trickles down to affect Blacks in the lower levels, who then discriminate against each other. In one complicated civil-rights case, still pending, charges of race discrimination were leveled against a White female supervisor by a Black woman in middle management, who in turn was charged with color discrimination by a lighter-skinned Black female subordinate. The light-skinned woman claimed that when she transferred to the department her supervisor informed her, ''You'll have it easy here. They like your type.'' After a few months the medium-toned supervisor demoted the light-skinned employee and moved her into a department where she was supervised by an even darker-skinned Black woman. The new supervisor repeatedly reprimanded her for displaying what the employee considered normal social behavior and eventually dismissed her. In both cases, the light-skinned woman felt she was being harassed because of her color.

Much color harassment in the workplace clearly stems from the larger societal problem of institutionalized racism. Yet Blacks may find it far easier to lodge a complaint of racism than of colorism. Blacks who challenge racism are supported not only by their own community but also by those Whites who are ashamed of their racist peers. But Black employees who encounter color harassment may decide to do nothing, even though psychologically the consequences can be just as damaging. Color divides the Black community, but the pressure to keep quiet about it is enormous. Few African Americans are willing to subject themselves to the kind of criticism inflicted upon Tracy Morrow during her color-discrimination suit: ''Why would she want to embarrass the Black community this way? She's just a high yella bitch. Is she looking for attention, or what?''

In the name of solidarity, Blacks too often have been reluctant to confront color prejudice in the workplace. Victims of intraracial color discrimination need to be able to feel that they can file complaints without censure. We do not wish to promote divisiveness in the Black community, but we feel that complaints of job-related color harassment deserve greater recognition by the public and greater respectability in the courts.

9. The Media: Images in Black and Light

"Michael, if it don't matter if you Black or White,
then why you White?"
—QUEEN SHENEQUA, "Weekend Update,"
  Saturday Night Live, 1991

From news coverage to entertainment, the media shape and reflect, reinforce and define, the world in which we live. In publishing, theater, films, television, and popular music—industries largely controlled by Whites—African Americans have struggled both for a voice and for fair representation. Much has been said and written about the racial stereotyping of Blacks in the media, but less attention has been paid to the role of skin color. Yet look closely at the Black women who play romantic leads in films: they nearly always have light skin and long hair. Light-skinned Black women with classic European features also predominate in beauty pageants, music videos, and the world of modeling. On the other hand, the Black men appearing in films today are mainly dark skinned, and Black actors who are light are often turned down for roles that call for virility, menace, or sexiness. Then there is the "king of pop," Michael Jackson, who has established his primacy in music videos, where image is everything. Jackson has undergone so much surgery that he hardly looks Black anymore. In our media-driven culture, print and visual imagery inevitably mirror and promote the same color prejudices that are found in our larger society.

Historically, this has long been the case. In nineteenth-century literature, color was crucial to the characterizations of Blacks, especially women. When portrayed as the love interest of either a Black or a White man, the Black heroine was typically light skinned, beautiful, and passive. In stories that were full of coincidence and ironic twists of fate, these heroines nearly always met a tragic end. In fact, the conflicts and downfalls associated with light-skinned Black females were so common in such novels that this stock character became known as the "tragic mulatta."

Today, literary critics speculate as to why the mulatta tragedy was such a popular genre. One theory holds that White females, the main reading audience for romantic fiction then and now, saw the mulatta through a veil of resentment. Southern White women, in particular, had felt victimized by their husbands' raping of slave women, but, being ladies, they had had to look the other way. Stories featuring mulattas may have offered this segment of the population a way tacitly to acknowledge the unsavory history of plantation rape; but the mulatta heroines had to die tragically, lest the stories appear to sanction miscegenation. In the North, and in the South after the Civil War, the stories may have served another purpose. The mulatta represented the vanguard of a fully integrated society, and stories about her tragic downfall might have helped soothe White anxieties about unchecked mixing of the races.

A related argument is that only racially mixed Blacks were thought worthy of White readers' attention. Full-blooded Negroes, especially women, were considered less complex and interesting and therefore did not lend themselves to convincingly tragic tales. Thus, in Harriet Beecher Stowe's classic *Uncle Tom's Cabin* (1852), the fugitive Liza and the rebellious Cassy are portrayed as mulatto, while Uncle Tom, the only pure Black, is a paragon of Christian submissiveness.

Another nineteenth-century White author of novels set in the Old South, George Washington Cable, wrote a book called *Old Creole Days* (1879), which centers around the beautiful octoroons of New Orleans, some of whom become the mistresses of rich White men. So frequently did nineteenth-century writers depict octoroons as delicate beauties that the word itself began to conjure up images of passive femininity. Although by definition an octoroon was either a male or a female with one-eighth Black blood, Black men in novels were rarely described as such. In fact, Black men were usually portrayed as dark-skinned brutes, since a sexually appealing portrayal of a Black man, especially a portrayal involving interracial love, would have been far too threatening for most White readers. Only the racially mixed Black female could be the object of Whites' fantasies and curiosity.

Successful nineteenth-century White writers knew that it was necessary to taint their mulattas' characters in such a way as to preclude their full participation in and acceptance into White society. The literary critic Sterling A. Brown points out that White stereotypes of mulattoes rested on a number of racist assumptions.

> First, the mulatto inherits the vices of both races and none of the virtues; second, any achievement of a Negro is to be attributed to the White blood in his veins. The logic runs that even inheriting the worst from Whites is sufficient for achieving among Negroes. . . . The mulatto is a victim of a divided inheritance; from his White blood come his intellectual strivings, his unwillingness to be a slave; from his Negro blood come his baser emotional urges, his indolence, his savagery.

Mulatta heroines were equally popular with early Black fiction writers, although for different reasons. First, early American Black writers were themselves usually mulatto, and writers generally write about what they know best. Second, mulattas provided a convenient illustration of the injustices of slave rape and racism. Finally, portraying mulattas who were light enough to pass gave the writer an opportunity to explore the question of allegiance to the Black race.

The earliest published novel by an American Negro included elements of the tragic mulatta figure. The author was a former slave, William Wells Brown, who fled to England, with the help of a Quaker family, and published his novel, *Clotel,* there in 1853. The book centers on the lives of three mulatta women, a mother and the two daughters she had by a White man, who later abandons them. It ends with a gang of Whites chasing one of the daughters, Clotel, who, unable to escape, drowns in the Potomac River within sight of Thomas Jefferson's White House.

The first novel by a Black writer to be published in America, however, transcended such melodramatic depictions of mulattas. Harriet

Wilson's *Our Nig* was published in Boston in 1859. Seemingly destined for obscurity, it was reissued in 1983 with an introduction by the Black scholar Henry Louis Gates, Jr. Wilson's plot is highly unusual for its era. Perhaps because she was not writing for a White audience but for Blacks (*Our Nig,* in fact, opens with an appeal for the patronage of "her colored brethren"), her mulatta heroine, Frado, is neither tragic nor apologetic. Frado's relations with White men are more pragmatic than romantic, and her oppressor, a White woman, suffers a slow and agonizing death. A Black man named Jim, moreover, becomes an equal partner in a marriage to a White woman. Wilson's failure to conform to the conventional literary treatment of Black characters may have been one reason why her remarkable novel was not better received. When the book was first released it was not even reviewed.

Another nineteenth-century Black female author, Frances Ellen Watkins Harper, fared better. In her novel, *Iola Leroy, or Shadows Uplifted* (generally thought to have been released in 1895, though some scholars date its publication as early as 1888), a fair-skinned mulatta heroine named Iola meets and falls in love with an aristocratic White doctor. When he discovers her true ancestry, he decides he loves her anyway and suggests that they run away to a place where no one will know the difference. The heroine at first considers the White man's offer, but in the end turns him down, concerned about leaving her family and about the fate of the mulatto children she might bear. In having Iola remain true to her race, Harper makes a clear statement about Black loyalty. At the same time, White readers could approve of Iola's refusal to indulge in miscegenation.

The turn-of-the-century Black writer Charles W. Chesnutt also dwelled on the tragic consequences attending the lives of mulattoes, but, unlike others before him, he created a positive portrait of a racially mixed Black man passing as White. In his *House Behind the Cedars* (1900), a mulatto named John Walden marries a White woman and fathers a child by her. Things go so well for him that he returns to his childhood home and persuades his younger sister, Rena, to move in with them so that she, too, can pass as White and improve her lot in life. Rena attracts the attentions of a White southern lawyer, and he, not knowing her true racial identity, asks for her hand in marriage. Then, through a series of accidents, he discovers her deception and breaks off the engagement, only to realize that he loves Rena after all. She dies in a tragic accident. The tragic flaw is not hers, however, but that of the White man, who learns too late that love transcends race.

By the 1920s a large number of Black artists and intellectuals had gathered in New York and were producing a virtual explosion and celebration of Afro-centered music, art, and literature. The energy of that era, known as the Harlem Renaissance, was fueled by an economic boom, the social agitation of both Negroes and women, and the "Great Migration" of southern Blacks to the North. While thousands of books, plays, and poems came out of the Harlem Renaissance, Black authors and artists still needed the approval of Whites to get their work published or produced. Melodramatic stories about tragic mulattoes were a tried-and-true theme, and many of the Harlem Renaissance writers continued to write in this genre.

Nella Larsen's *Quicksand* (1928) and *Passing* (1929) both depicted beautiful mulatta heroines struggling with their racial identity and their place in society. Like Larsen herself, these characters were educated and solidly middle-class in their values. Larsen's father was Black and her mother Danish, as are the parents of Helga, the protagonist of *Quicksand*. Novelist Jessie Fauset, too, wrote about mulattas in two works of fiction, *Plum Bun* (1928) and *There Is Confusion* (1924). Like many writers of the Harlem Renaissance, Fauset was light skinned and had pursued a higher education, earning an M.A. from Cornell University and studying at the Sorbonne in Paris. The fascination with mulatto characters for writers like Fauset and Larsen undoubtedly stemmed from their own social experiences.

It was also during the Harlem Renaissance that Black writers began to reflect seriously on the issue of color prejudice within the Negro community. Some, like George Schulyer, the author of *Black No More* (1931), felt free enough in their writing to satirize the subject of color and race; Wallace Thurman, in *The Blacker the Berry* (1929), dared to poke fun at a Black woman who was miserably unhappy because of her skin color. Thurman challenged members of his own race, as well as Whites, to dispel ignorance about discrimination. At a gathering of Harlem intellectuals, a character he called Truman declares:

"Then consider that the mulatto is much nearer white than he is black, and is therefore more liable to act like a white man than like a black one, although I cannot say that I see a great deal of difference in any of their actions. They are human beings first and only white or black incidentally."

The noted Harlem Renaissance poet and author Langston Hughes was another who explored the psychology of color from the Black perspective. Hughes wrote a number of stories, essays, and plays, including a drama called *Mulatto* (1935), that address issues of color and race. *Mulatto,* which enjoyed a successful run on Broadway from 1935 to 1937, concerns illicit relationships in the South and centers on the conflict between a mulatto son and his White father. Some of Hughes's poems also deal with race mixing, including "Cross," the last verse of which served as the epigraph to Nella Larsen's *Quicksand.*

My old man died in a fine big house.
My ma died in a shack.
I wonder where I'm going to die.
Being neither white nor black.

In another poem, "Harlem Sweeties," Hughes celebrated skin color differences among African-American women in his Sugar Hill neighborhood.

Have you dug the spill
Of Sugar Hill?
Cast your gims
On this sepia thrill:
Brown sugar lassie,
Caramel treat,

Honey-gold baby
Sweet enough to eat.
Peach-skin girlie,
Coffee and cream,
Chocolate darling
Out of a dream.
. . . .

Caramel, brown sugar,
A chocolate treat.
Molasses taffy,
Coffee and cream,
Licorice, clove, cinnamon
To a honey-brown dream.
Cinnamon, honey brown dream.
Ginger, wine gold
Persimmon, blackberry,
All through the spectrum
Harlem girls vary—
So if you want to know beauty's
Rainbow-sweet thrill,
Stroll down luscious,
Delicious, fine Sugar Hill.

Gwendolyn Brooks—perhaps the most celebrated Black American poet—directly confronted intraracial discrimination in some of her later work. In "The Ballad of Chocolate Mabbie" (1944), Brooks captures a Black child's initial awareness of color prejudice. The poem relates the tale of dark-skinned Mabbie, who discovers that her boyfriend, Willie, prefers a girl who is lighter. The first verse goes:

It was Mabbie without the grammar school gates.
And Mabbie was all of seven.
And Mabbie was cut from a chocolate bar.
And Mabbie thought life was heaven.

Later, we feel sorry for the joyous Mabbie when she spies her young beau holding hands with her long-haired rival.

> *Out came the saucily bold Willie Boone.*
> *It was woe for our Mabbie now.*
> *He wore like a jewel a lemon-hued lynx*
> *With sand-waves loving her brow.*

Many writers of the late Renaissance wrote for Blacks without worrying about whether Whites would understand or approve. Two 1930s novels by Zora Neale Hurston are conspicuously free of any White characters. *Jonah's Gourd Vine* (1934) tells the story of a mulatto preacher whose illicit love affairs lead to his self-destruction, and *Their Eyes Were Watching God* (1937) describes the trials and tribulations of a mulatta named Janie in an all-Black community in Florida. In both works, the mulatto protagonists' lives are complicated by the color complexes of others.

In the literary arena, at least, Blacks had the freedom to explore their own voices and to exercise some creative control. The same could not be said for other media outlets, especially the theater and motion pictures. Traditional color prejudices would prevail on the stage and the silver screen for several more decades.

During the twenties, Harlem set the world to dancing, and the Black musical emerged as a new theatrical form. Negro singing and dancing were suddenly in great demand, by White and Black audiences alike. Yet the casting of women in the chorus lines continued to cater to fantasies of "exotic octoroon girls," as these White-looking dancers were often billed.

Among the greatest and most widely known of Harlem entertainers was Josephine Baker. Although sometimes described as light skinned, Baker was considered not "quite light enough" when she auditioned for Eubie Blake's and Nobel Sissle's Black musical, *Shuffle Along* (1921). The director said that her "dark" skin would not fit in with that of the "high yella girls" and offered her the job of dresser instead. One fateful evening, one of the regular chorus girls did not appear, and Baker, who had memorized the steps from watching the show backstage, convinced the director to let her go on. To the other girls' dismay, the crowd adored the newcomer, and Baker became a permanent cast member of *Shuffle Along,* one of the most successful Negro musicals ever to run in New York. Baker later went to Europe, where she mesmerized audiences in Paris and elsewhere with her beauty, charm, humor, and flirtatious sensuality. She became known as "the girl who put Harlem on the map of Europe." Ironically, the attribute that had initially held Baker back in her own country—her medium-brown skin color—contributed to her success abroad. Yet despite Baker's obvious appeal, the directors of other Black American musicals, including *Hot Chocolates* (1929) and *Chocolate Dandies* (1925), continued to hire only chorus girls with white or near-white skin. It was commonly believed that dark-skinned girls would offend middle-class White and Black patrons alike.

Despite such color prejudice, these musicals represented a vast expansion of opportunities for Black stage performers. Only two decades before, minstrel shows had been featuring Negro actors in blackface portraying shiftless drunks addicted to watermelon and chicken, usually stolen. In addition to this demeaning "coon-like" image of Blacks, there were two other common stage stereotypes, the brute and the tragic mulatta. The brute was nearly always a dark-skinned male, and one White playwright, Eugene Walter, in his drama *The Easiest Way,* described even a mammy part as "cunning, crafty, heartless, sullen. . . . The actress who plays this part must keep in mind its innate and brutal selfishness." As they traditionally had in literature, the mulatta and brute characterizations of Negroes in theater and later in film functioned to alleviate Whites' anxieties about rampant race mixing while maintaining the myth of White superiority.

Film directors simply imitated and extended such stereotypic depictions of Blacks. According to African-American film scholar Donald Bogle, during Hollywood's early years directors seemed able to cast Black actors and actresses (or Whites in blackface) in only five basic roles—the Tom (as personified by Bill "Bojangles" Robinson), the coon (Stepin Fetchit), the Black buck (Paul Robeson), the mammy (Louise Beavers), and, of course, the tragic mulatta (Fredi

Washington). The Black men who played these stereotyped roles were mostly medium brown skinned, and if a director considered them not dark enough, they were simply smeared with blackface. For women, however, skin color was a critical factor in casting: light-skinned Black actresses were given sympathetic and sexually charged roles; women who were dark were cast as mammies.

One of the first films to exploit these two sharply delineated roles for Black women was D. W. Griffith's controversial *Birth of a Nation* (1915). The NAACP found the film so offensive that it picketed the New York premiere, and riots broke out when the film opened in Boston and Chicago. Eventually it was banned in five states and nineteen cities. Ironically, the roles of the sensual tragic mulatta, Lydia, and of the dark-skinned, overweight mammy were both played by White actresses in blackface.

Playing on racist fears about the uncontrollable sexuality of Black men, *Birth of a Nation* also perpetuated the buck or brute stereotype. In one episode a very dark skinned Black man (actually a White man in blackface) attempts to defile a White southern woman, whose rescue by the KKK is sympathetically depicted.

Seven years later, Griffith re-created another stereotypic stage role, that of the cowardly but funny Negro frightened to death by his own shadow, in a film called *One Exciting Night* (1922). Again a White man in blackface played the part in the Griffith film, but throughout the 1920s and 1930s a Black actor, Stepin Fetchit, came to epitomize this sexless, buffoonish type of character in the roles he played. (Unlike the shuffling, laconic character he often played on-screen, Fetchit worked hard off screen to eliminate segregation in the film industry.)

In 1915, a group of Black actors and investors had moved to counter some of the film stereotypes by forming their own film company, the Lincoln Motion Picture Company, in Los Angeles. The light-skinned actor Noble Johnson was the company's first president. This little-known organization produced a number of films, including *The Realization of a Negro's Ambition* and *The Trooper of Company K,* for and about Blacks. Reflecting the life-styles of the company's Black bourgeois backers, however, the casting was restricted to light-skinned Blacks, usually in middle-class roles. Some of the actors who appeared in these silent black-and-white films were so light skinned that it was difficult to tell they were Black. By 1923 the Lincoln Motion Picture Company had gone under, a victim of poor distribution and perhaps of the obstacles faced by those who attempted to challenge stereotypes of Blacks in the media.

Black production companies seemed to fare better if they stuck to traditional melodrama. Such was the case with a film called *The Scar of Shame* (1927), produced by the Colored Players Film Production (which, though White owned, was formed to make films about Blacks). The plot centers on a lower-class mulatta named Louise Howard, who escapes from her brute father by marrying an aspiring middle-class Black composer named Alvin. Louise's gambler father arranges for a man named Eddie to kidnap her and bring her back, but the plan goes awry; she is accidentally wounded in the neck in a pistol fight between Eddie and Alvin, who is trying to save her. With her beauty marred (the scar of shame) and Alvin in prison, Louise turns to prostitution. After Alvin's release Louise tries to win back his love, but when that fails she commits suicide, leaving Alvin free to marry a woman of his own social standing. The film, produced with the financial backing of the Black bourgeoisie, offers a stern warning about marrying outside one's social caste. An analysis of *The Scar of Shame* by the film scholar Jane Gaines explores its subversive message about color.

The Scar of Shame is not able to speak about its own subtle racism or about the racism in the Black film industry in the 1920s. On the screen the actors playing Louise, Alvin, Alice, and the baser element, Eddie, appear exactly the same degree of light brown. The actor playing Spike, Louise's father, seems darker than the other actors (with the exceptions of the inhabitants of the local bar).

Gaines goes on to note that much of the colorism apparent in early White films tended to be the reverse of the color bias operating in Black films.

That is, light-skinned Blacks could not find work in White motion pictures. Black and white film stock registered too much truth—on the screen racially mixed actors looked White. Conversely, the dark-skinned Blacks preferred by White producers were unacceptable in star roles in race films. They were not idealized (i.e., White) enough.

The best-known early Black filmmaker was Oscar Micheaux. Like others of his era, he cast exclusively light-skinned Black actors and actresses in the more than twenty silent and sound movies he made. Micheaux's first film, *The Homesteader* (1919), was adapted from his semiautobiographical novel of the same name, and he financed it by selling stock in his own film company. Before his career ended Micheaux had worked the cinematic spectrum, from Chesnutt's *The House Behind the Cedars,* which he adapted and filmed in 1923, to the genre known as "ghetto films," which flooded the market from the 1930s through the 1950s. Cheaply made and usually shot by Black directors, "ghetto films" featured light-skinned Blacks in ridiculous Western and gangster roles. While these grade-B films gave some Black actors their start, most longed to appear in the bigger and more respectable Hollywood releases. With the exception of the usual stock characters, however, few Black actresses and even fewer actors were able to land decent parts, and so they took what they could get.

By the 1930s the Black mammy character had emerged as a staple in White commercial films. Most people today probably think of Hattie McDaniel as the definitive mammy for her Oscar-winning performance in *Gone With the Wind* (1939), but the brown-skinned Louise Beavers had personified the role well before then. Beavers received critical acclaim for her mammy character in the melodramatic *Imitation of Life* (1934), in which the white-skinned Black actress Fredi Washington played the part of Beavers's tormented light-skinned daughter. In this classic tragic-mulatta tale, a light-skinned girl grows up in a White household and is the best friend of the White daughter of the woman for whom her mother works. In one tearful scene after another the mulatta daughter denies and abandons her dark-skinned mother so that others will think she is White, like her childhood friend.

In the end Beavers's long-suffering mammy character dies before her daughter can apologize for her actions.

Black moviegoers had varying reactions to this film; some enjoyed it, but most thought that it reinforced the old stereotypes of Black women as either tragic or passive. Despite its commercial success, the film did not particularly help the careers of either Beavers or Washington. While Beavers went on to star in other films, her salary never increased, nor did she get very far beyond maid roles. And White directors considered Washington too light except for parts requiring someone light enough to pass (yet not romantically involved with anyone White).

Passing was a popular theme of several Hollywood releases of the forties and fifties. *Lost Boundaries* (1949) was based on a true story about a doctor and his family who pass as White during the depression. All goes well until the doctor attempts to volunteer for the navy, just before Pearl Harbor, and is exposed as Black. The film is fairly sympathetic in its treatment of the doctor and his family—the scene in which he reveals to his children that they are not White is especially moving—and Black audiences generally approved of it. In contrast, *Pinky* (1949) resorted to the usual simplistic stereotypes. A tragic mulatta (actually played by a White woman) falls in love with a White doctor and flees in confusion when he proposes marriage. She returns to the home of her dark-skinned mammy-like grandmother, who urges her to become the private nurse of a rich, elderly White woman. When the old woman dies, the dutiful light-skinned granddaughter inherits all her money. Society's and Hollywood's obsession with the tragic mulatta was again reflected in a 1959 remake of *Imitation of Life,* starring Juanita Moore as the mammy-mother and White actress Susan Kohner as the tragic-mulatta daughter. The film was so melodramatic that Black audiences often burst out laughing during the extravagant funeral scene, in which the mulatta daughter hysterically throws herself on her mother's coffin. The message of these films was none too subtle: if you do not mix races, you will be generously rewarded; if you try to pass as White, tragedy awaits.

The frequent casting of White rather than Black actresses in the tragic-mulatta roles reflected Hollywood's discomfort with interracial romance. In fact, the Code of the Motion Picture Industry, a rigid and often ridiculous system of self-censorship, prohibited any on-screen sexual (that is, romantic) contact between a White and a Black actor and actress. This left very light-skinned actresses, like Fredi Washington and Lena Horne, with hardly any available parts. The code was not relaxed until the late 1950s.

When Lena Horne signed with MGM in the early forties, studio executives were not sure what to do with her. Since she had already achieved fame as a singer, she was able to have her contract stipulate that she was not to be cast as a maid or a jungle type. Yet on her first screen test the casting directors thought that she looked too White in comparison to the Black actor Eddie Anderson (who later became famous as Rochester, Jack Benny's comic sidekick). In the family biography *The Hornes,* Lena's daughter, Gail Lumet Buckley, describes what happened next.

> So much dark make-up was smeared on Lena's face in an attempt to match her skin color to Rochester's that she began to look like Al Jolson singing "Mammy." At that point Max Factor himself was summoned to confront the problem. How could they make Lena look black, but not blacked up? The Factors chemists soon came up with a coppery-caramel-colored pancake make-up, to be applied to the skin with a wet sponge. It did wonders for Hedy Lamarr in *White Cargo,* a part that Lena longed for.

Because Hollywood never did figure out how to type her, Horne ended up playing herself, a lounge singer, in her first two films, *Cabin in the Sky* (1942) and *Stormy Weather* (1943).

Finally, with *Island in the Sun* (1957), Hollywood lifted its ban on interracial love affairs, allowing the portrayal of two such relationships: one with Black actress Dorothy Dandridge playing the love interest of a White man and the other, even more scandalous, featuring a Black man, Harry Belafonte, in love with a rich White woman, Joan Fontaine. Still, no kissing was shown; there was one quick embrace between Dandridge and her White boyfriend but virtually no physical contact between Belafonte and Fontaine.

During the fifties and sixties Hollywood began offering Black actors and actresses somewhat more complex and varied roles, but dark-skinned Black men continued to be cast as brutes or, if, like Sidney Poitier, they were sympathetically portrayed, they were "desexed." Poitier achieved fame in a string of hit films, including *The Blackboard Jungle* (1955), *Raisin in the Sun* (1961), *Lilies of the Field* (1963), *To Sir with Love* (1967), and *Guess Who's Coming to Dinner* (1967). Poitier's parts varied tremendously from film to film, but his characters were often impossibly virtuous and hardly Black. Even in *Guess Who's Coming to Dinner,* a film about interracial love, Poitier's character was so deracinated that one angry Black writer called him a "warmed-over white shirt."

The seventies marked the appearance of what would later be called the genre of "blaxploitation"—films that portrayed Black males as inner-city thugs who made a living pimping women or selling drugs. Between 1970 and 1992 fifty such movies were made, *Superfly* and *Shaft* being the best known. Although "blaxploitation" films gave Black men more interesting and dynamic roles than had previously been open to them, the films tended to revive the old association between dark-skinned men and violence. With the exception of actor Ron O'Neal, who played Superfly, most of the Black actors starring in these films were quite dark.

During the late seventies and the eighties Richard Pryor and Eddie Murphy emerged as major box-office attractions. In spite of being relatively dark skinned, they did not have to play the kind of morally superior roles that Poitier did in order to gain respectability. It was their humor that disarmed them and made them acceptable to the general public.

Today, Murphy and many other Black actors, including Denzel Washington, Lou Gossett, Jr., Morgan Freeman, Danny Glover, and Wesley Snipes, enjoy celebrity status with Black and White audiences alike, and as a result have acquired power in Hollywood. As actors, they express a wide range of emotions in dramas as well as comedies, and often play roles in which their race is an integral part of their on-screen characters, not an incidental factor. Yet skin color remains an issue in Hollywood casting. Most of the Black males who get steady work in commercial films today have medium to dark skin, and those who are light complain that they rarely land good parts. Except for the rare middle-class Black role, light skin has become a definite disadvantage for males when it comes to casting. As one light-skinned actor commented:

> I often play buppie and corporate executive types, roles perfectly acceptable for light-skinned Black men. My skin color has also helped me get nontraditional parts that don't necessarily require a Black actor. In one play, I even had a wife who was White, but it was okay because I was light-skinned. I have a harder time getting traditional roles for Blacks, though, because I'm not "dark" enough. So I usually only get calls for young dads, corporate types, and toothpaste commercials.

Several Black actors and directors have remarked that the recent trend of nontraditional casting (putting Blacks in White parts) in the theater is helping light-skinned actors get parts but that film directors are generally more conservative.

For a brief period in the early seventies some of the same color biases that affected the casting of Black men were applied to very light skinned Black women. Debra Pratt, a writer, director, and actress, was told after one audition that she was inappropriate for the lead because it required "a real Black woman," and she didn't "really look Black enough." More recently, though, light-skinned Black actresses are again the preferred romantic love interest in major commercial films. It is apparently an inviolate rule in Hollywood that Black actresses—Appolonia in *Purple Rain,* Vanity in *Action Jackson,* Shari Headley in *Coming to America,* Cynda Williams in *Mo' Better Blues,* Halle Berry in *Strictly Business,* Lonette McKee in *Jungle Fever*—are always lighter than their Black leading men.

Lighter-skinned Black actresses are also preferred for the few roles involving interracial liaisons. The racially mixed Rae Dawn Chong has been cast opposite some of Hollywood's best-known White leading men, including Michael Keaton *(The Squeeze)*, Arnold Schwarzenegger *(Commando)*, Keith Carradine *(Choose Me)*, and Kevin Costner *(American Flyers)*. When asked why she is so often chosen to play interracial love interests, Chong responds that it is because she is "not so dark."

The film industry's reluctance to cast dark-skinned Black women in romantic leads applies even to the most successful Black actress working in Hollywood today, Whoopi Goldberg. Despite her huge box-office draw, most directors consider her unsuitable as a love interest. In fact, a love scene between Goldberg and her White co-star, Sam Elliot, that was shot for the film *Fatal Beauty* ended up on the cutting-room floor. Like Hattie McDaniel, Goldberg has been recognized by the Academy of Motion Picture Arts and Sciences for her acting talent, yet her roles are restricted because of her dark skin and natural hair.

Today, however, African Americans are more likely to be found behind the camera. Black directors like Spike Lee *(Do The Right Thing, Mo' Better Blues, Jungle Fever,* and *Malcolm X)*, Euzhan Palcy *(A Dry White Season)*, Robert Townsend *(Hollywood Shuffle* and *The Five Heartbeats)*, Keenan Ivory Wayans *(I'm Gonna Git You Sucka)*, Mario Van Peebles *(New Jack City)*, John Singleton *(Boyz N the Hood* and *Poetic Justice)*, Matty Rich *(Straight Out of Brooklyn)*, and Julie Dash *(Daughters of the Dusk)* are gaining power and creative control. A more Afrocentric perspective on various social issues, including skin color and interracial relationships, is being brought to the screen. It is hard, if not impossible, to imagine a White male director filming a story about interracial love that depicts the outrage of Black women as Lee did in the so-called "war council" scene in *Jungle Fever*. And independent women directors, like Debra Robinson, Michelle Parkenson, and Zeinabu irene Davis, undoubtedly will bring yet another spin to the subject. Davis claims that she makes a deliberate effort in her films to "reject Hollywood's status quo notions of what Black women are supposed to look like." In her latest release, *A Powerful Thang*, she cast a medium-brown-skinned Black woman with long dreadlocks as the romantic lead.

On the television screen, Black actors and actresses have had to battle similar racial prejudices, but in some ways skin color has been less of an issue. With the exception of *Amos 'n' Andy* (1951 – 1966), in which dark-skinned characters embodied the traditional buffoonish stereotypes, most of the Blacks who appeared during the "golden years" of television were singers and dancers on variety shows. These performers were featured in all their various skin colors. There is no question that Blacks have been underrepresented in television, but in weekly sitcoms and drama shows like *I Spy,* with Bill Cosby, *Julia,* with Diahann Carroll, *The Jeffersons, Good Times,* and *Sanford and Son,* up to the recent *Cosby Show, A Different World, Family Matters,* and *Fresh Prince of Bel Air,* skin color has not been a big factor in casting. One explanation might be that television is a more democratic medium than film. People do not have to pay to see it, and since it enters viewers' homes, many of the shows strive to create characters who are "just folks." Or it may be that the film industry is more conservative because producing a movie requires a much larger investment of time and money, or because the silver screen is reserved for larger-than-life epic dramas, idealized romances, and action adventures. Finally, it may be that Blacks on television are viewed more as entertainers than actors. For instance, while talk-show hosts Oprah Winfrey and Arsenio Hall have both acted in films, their reputations are based on their popular television shows. Finally, the television industry may simply be more sensitive to the color issue. Bill Cosby's *A Different World,* in particular, appears to make a concerted effort to cast African-American actors and actresses with a range of skin colors in a variety of different roles.

Television is also host to annual beauty pageants whose winners provide one measure of society's views regarding the attractiveness of Black women. Because of discrimination in the beauty-pageant industry, Blacks have traditionally held their own pageants, with contestants displaying a wide range of color and features. In 1983, however, the green-eyed, light-skinned Vanessa Williams became the first Black woman to be crowned Miss America. While Williams is perhaps best remembered by the White public for her nude photos in *Penthouse,* her winning generated a different kind of controversy among Blacks. The Congress of Racial Equality (CORE) went so far as to issue a statement declaring Williams not "in essence Black"—a comment that deeply hurt her. When *Chicago Tribune* columnist Leanita McClain wrote favorably about Williams's victory, she was swamped with calls and letters from angry Blacks. In a second column, entitled "Beauty Brings Out the Beast," McClain reviewed this response.

> "Of course, they'd pick her," said one caller, referring to the crowning of Vanessa Williams, 20, of Milwood, N.Y., the first black to win the title Miss America, "she's the least black-looking person they could find." . . . Another unnerved caller remarked, "Why did they pick someone so fair that they had to ask her if she was half-white?"

Herself a light-skinned woman, McClain called the Black community to task for its color prejudice.

> Those people who choose to feel superior or inferior to others of their own race on the basis of skin color ought to spend more time looking over themselves. Whatever happened to the message of "black is beautiful," to the thinking that blacks were a melting pot all to themselves, to the poetry that celebrated shades from honey to ebony? . . . There will always be people—black and white—with acute cases of color consciousness, individuals concerned about how light or how dark someone's complexion is, how straight or how kinky someone's hair is. But the bottom line is black is black, off-white is black and so is every color in between.

Less than a year later, McClain committed suicide, for reasons that some believe were related to her unresolved conflicts about being a light-skinned middle-class Black in a position of having to speak for the racial experiences of others.

Since William's victory, Black women have been winning major beauty awards at an astonishing rate. In 1990, African-American women reigned as Miss USA (Carole Gist) and Miss America (Debbye

Turner), and for the first time a Black woman was selected as *Playboy*'s "Playmate of the Year." In 1991, yet another African-American woman, Marjorie Judith Vincent, was crowned Miss America. While these "Black beauties" all wear their hair straight and could not by any stretch of the imagination be considered Afrocentric in style or appearance, neither are they uniformly light skinned, fine featured, or light eyed.

Beautiful Black women are also enjoying high-powered careers as models. Skin color matters in the fickle world of modeling, but it matters in less predictable ways. Who makes it and who doesn't is determined by two opposing forces, one conservative and the other progressive. On the conservative side are the advertising agencies, along with the corporations they represent, who prefer mainstream-looking models. On the other side are the internationally renowned fashion designers, who want their models to look exotic. Strongly African-looking women, including the singer actress Grace Jones, the Somalian-born Iman, the African-Jamaicanized Naomi Campbell, and Roshumba, whose signature is a closely cropped Afro, successfully work the runways at shows in New York, Paris, Milan, and Rome. While these Black women have made their mark, and a great deal of money, in the fast-paced glamour of high fashion, they have not been immune to criticism. Campbell has been accused of "compromising" her heritage by wearing "platinum and honey-blond wigs"—to her just another accessory—and Roshumba is considered "difficult" because she refuses to wear such wigs.

Dark-skinned Black women flipping through the pages of such high-fashion magazines as *Vogue, Harper's Bazaar, Mademoiselle,* and *Elle* are undoubtedly cheered to see page after page of dark-skinned supermodels like Iman and Naomi Campbell. However, when it comes to promoting everyday products, light-skinned models like Shari Belafonte and Kara Young are still the rule. A model like Belafonte can work both in high fashion and, because of her light skin and all-American looks, in the lucrative commercial market. But someone like Grace Jones is unlikely to be chosen to sell Fords or even Calvin Klein jeans, and many advertisers doubt that any dark-skinned Black woman, no matter how beautiful, can effectively sell their products.

Bethann Hardison, a former model for Black designer Stephen Borrows and the owner and manager of the New York–based modeling agency Bethann Management Co., says, "Color is like a fashion. It just depends on what people want at the time. Sometimes when a company desires a clear visual difference in their ad, they'll ask for a Black model who is definitely Black looking."

On the other hand, racism can sometimes prevent very light skinned Black models from getting work. One beautiful Black woman with light skin, keen features, and long straight hair has passed as White in order to keep certain modeling assignments. As she explains:

> An agency will call me up, all excited. But when I get there the questions start. They ask, "What are you?" "I am Black," I reply. "Black and what else?" they inquire. "I am Black, Black, just Black. That's all, nothing else." Then they go into the back office for a moment and come back out saying, "Thank you for coming, but you're not exactly what we're looking for." So I've gotten smart, and I just pass as Greek, Italian, or Latin. Now they love me. I'm exotic. I've even got a national fur campaign from a company that specifically didn't want Blacks. Joke's on them.

The underutilization of Black models is evident in the number registered with New York's top agencies. Out of more than 200 models associated with Elite Model Management in 1991, only 14 were Black; of the 180 models with the Ford Modeling Agency, only 8 were Black; among the 124 models working at Wilhelmina, only 12 were Black. These agencies would undoubtedly sign more Black women if there were a greater demand for them from advertisers.

The extent of racism and colorism in advertising was fully documented in a 1991 report entitled *Invisible People* issued by the Department of Consumer Affairs of New York. It tallied the number of Black models appearing in over 11,000 ads in 27 different national magazines, along with descriptions of the models' physical appearance and how they were positioned in each ad. While approximately 11 percent of the magazines' readership was Black, over 96 percent of the models were White. In addition, most of the Blacks in the ads appeared in group shots dominated by Whites, and the Black women were usually light skinned and had long, wavy hair.

The infrequency with which ads portray African Americans and the limited range of skin colors considered suitable for promoting everyday products say much about our society's willingness to accept Blacks into the mainstream culture. Nowhere is this bias more apparent than in advertising for cosmetics. Research by Linda Jackson and Kelly Ervin has found that such products are the least likely to be touted by Black women. While some beauty care and personal hygiene products are specifically designed and marketed for Black women, many others are used equally by both Whites and Blacks. One Black model, Cynthia Bailey, has observed from personal experience that Black models, especially dark-skinned ones like herself, are hardly ever hired to sell products that Whites might use. "Take hair spray, for example," she says. "You don't see Black girls in hair-spray commercials, yet we use just as much hair spray as White women. If you see a Black woman advertising hair spray, it's a Black hair-spray product being advertised on a Black television show at two o'clock in the morning after the airing of *Soul Train.*"

Some of the same issues that affect the careers of Black women in modeling also color the opportunities of Black male models. Most advertising agencies prefer them to be light skinned, with fine features and light eyes—"pretty boys" as far from tough and threatening looking as Black men can be in this society. In fact, some darker-skinned male models complain that it is harder for them to get work than it is for their dark-toned sisters, who at least stand a chance of being labeled "exotic." Dark skin on men, especially when combined with broad features, always seems to suggest that they are hard, mean, or poor.

It is unfortunate that industry-wide color bias limits the careers of individual Black models, but what is of greater concern is the long-term effect of color stereotyping in the popular media on the Black community. The self-esteem of dark-skinned Black women, in particular, is bound to suffer from the omnipresence of light-skinned women in commercial (as opposed to fashion) ads. Young Black men are less inclined to suffer in the same way, since fewer aspire to look like models.

Some experts in the field maintain that dark-skinned Blacks are rarely hired as models because dark skin is hard to photograph. It tends to "flatten out" under strong lighting or in bright sunlight, making it difficult to capture the subtle shapes of facial features. Lighting crews for video and film, as well as still photographers, readily confess to a preference for light-skinned Black subjects, particularly for outdoor shots.

Trudy Haynes, who in 1963 became the United States' first Black TV reporter and weathercaster and is now the entertainment reporter for KYW-TV's *Eyewitness News* in Philadelphia, points out that the skin of African Americans generally does have different undertones and that their hair may absorb light instead of reflecting it. Studio lighting is normally set for Whites and has to be adjusted for Blacks. In her experience, the bigger the name of a Black celebrity, the greater the effort that will be made to provide the proper lighting.

It may be lighting or it may be the old prejudice against dark skin that is responsible for the fact that many of the first Blacks in television news, including Haynes, Max Robinson (ABC), Carole Simpson (ABC), and George Strait (ABC), were light skinned. However, improved camera technology and a larger pool of Black television journalists from which to draw have led to the hiring of an increasing number of medium to darker-skinned Blacks as both anchors and field reporters.

In the eighties, television went cable, sound went video, and image and packaging began to rival talent and personality in the music industry. In today's world of MTV (Music Television), big concert films, and glitzy award shows, performers need great looks, universal sex appeal, and a certain marketable "spin" before they can capture the attention of record producers and the public.

Color and image were not always so important to the singing careers of Blacks. Some of the greatest blues, gospel, pop, jazz, and soul singers—Bessie Smith, Mahalia Jackson, Ella Fitzgerald, Sarah Vaughn, Pearl Bailey, Aretha Franklin—were dark and full figured. No matter how talented, these women would probably have a difficult time making it in today's image-driven music industry. The willowy and glamorous Whitney Houston, for example, has the look that sells, especially in the lucrative crossover pop-music market.

In comparison, many of the old great Black male singers—Billy Eckstine, Cab Calloway, Harry Belafonte, Nat "King" Cole, Sam Cooke—were dashing and/or light-skinned, and were full of easy smiles and charm. Given the brute image of Black men presented in the media, did these Negro musicians of the big-band era think they had to maintain a nonthreatening demeanor in order to attract a large White following? Perhaps, but, even so, they failed to capture a certain segment of the White market because they were Black. Thus, while big-band leaders like Benny Goodman and later Tommy Dorsey were certainly talented in their own right, much of their popularity rested on the fact that they were Whites imitating the innovative styles of Blacks. Later, another White man "borrowed heavily" from the Black blues musicians of Memphis and made it bigger than they ever had; music historians believe that Elvis Presley's primary appeal lay in his being a White man who "sang Black."

Distinctly Black and urban in origin, rap is the first music genre in which a Black man can be angry and intense and still sell records to Whites. In fact, the more a Black rapper evokes images of dangerous sexuality and criminal violence, the more his records seem to appeal to a White audience. Rap music made its debut along with MTV, BET (Black Entertainment Television), and VH1 (Video Hits), all of which are primarily watched by White suburban males. According to the pop-culture critic David Samuels, much of the appeal of rap music is that it gives Whites a controlled glimpse into a different culture. White stylists and record producers deliberately manipulated the images of some of the early groups, like Run-DMC and Public Enemy, to make them appear harder and tougher than they actually were. While acknowledging Public Enemy's musical innovations, Samuels comments that "the root of Public Enemy's success was a highly charged theatre of race in which white listeners became guilty eavesdroppers on the putative private conversation of the inner city.'' Behind the video images of the Black rappers, *Village Voice* critic Nelson George sees a ''ghettocentrism,'' a style-driven cult of Blackness marked by crude stereotypes, or, in other words, the image of the brute revisited.

The image of the octoroon beauty has also been resurrected in these videos. Rarely if ever are dark-skinned Black women with Negroid features and natural hair depicted in rap videos. Instead, long-haired Black women with Caucasian features strike provocative poses behind macho Black male rap artists. As the Harvard psychiatrist Alvin Poussaint has commented:

> The preference for light skin, long straight hair, and keen features comes through most strongly in music videos where dark-skinned Black men frequently choose light-skinned Black women with White features as love interests. Picking this type of woman as an emblem of beauty and desire is a class issue for many urban dark-skinned Black men.

Poussaint's analysis suggests that White producers are not necessarily to blame for the selection of lighter-skinned women in rap video. In fact, male rappers from Fresh Prince to Brotherhood Creed occasionally voice traditional color prejudices in their songs. Lines like ''Light-skin honeys of the red-bone breed. You got, you got, you got what I need'' (Big Daddy Kane) express familiar fantasies about light-skinned Black women.

Yet there are other contemporary Black musicians who are using their art form to challenge the stereotyped notion of ''lighter is righter.'' In a song entitled ''No Nose Job,'' the Black rap group Digital Underground is highly critical of Blacks who surgically alter their noses, and in a song entitled ''Dark Skin Girls,'' Rapper Del celebrates the joys of dark skin.

> *Dark-skinned girls are better than light skin.*
> *Light-skinned girls aren't better than dark skin.*

I can't understand you light skin winches
You think you're all that cause you have long extensions
Your hair was natural, now you played out rays.
You woulda looked better with a fade.

Next time you see a girl darker than you
No disrespect when you meet her
Cause the girl look better than you.

While these lyrics certainly do not play to the usual fantasies about light-skinned Black women, ultimately they go too far in demeaning women who happen to be light skinned.

Talented Black women rappers, like Queen Latifah, Salt N' Pepa, Sister Souljah, and BWP (Bytches With Problems), and the folk-rock singer Tracy Chapman are also challenging the color prejudices of the media with their strongly ethnic looks and Afrocentric styles. This new wave of female musicians is letting audiences know that Black women do not have to be light skinned and delicate to be considered beautiful and sexy.

Some believe Jermaine Jackson used the media in 1991 as a forum to criticize his brother Michael's "Aryan" transformation. On his album *You Said,* in a song called "Word to the Badd" (*Bad* happens to be the title of one of Michael's top-selling albums), Jermaine seems to lament the fact that once Michael had it made, he changed his shade.

This family has come far since the early seventies, when Michael, Jermaine, and three of their brothers burst onto the Black music scene in a group called the Jackson 5. With their darker skin, Negroid features, and large afros, as well as their style of dancing, singing, and music, the Jacksons were unmistakably Black.

Eventually Michael pulled away from his brothers to establish a solo career. In 1979 he became a megastar with his album *Off the Wall,* produced by Quincy Jones. His new style forever changed the music scene, but the music scene also forever changed Michael. His hair became less ethnic and more European looking; with the advent of the Jheri Curl, it was not unlike the hairstyles of many other Black men and women of the time. But then he slowly began to alter other features. His broad, unmistakably Negroid nose became narrow, his rounded chin became squared and clefted, and with each new album released, from *Thriller* to *Bad,* his dark skin seemed to become progressively paler. In what appeared to be a testament to his media savvy, Michael emerged from his persona as the youngest, cutest member of the Jackson 5 to the persona of an internationally recognizable Black superstar—with long, free-swinging hair, delicate features, and light skin.

Whether Michael Jackson's success was in any way connected to his less "threatening" appearance is debatable. And whether he lightened his skin color for cosmetic or for medical reasons (as his public relations people sometimes allege) is a matter between him and his doctor. But no one disputes the fact that Michael Jackson looks far less Black than he once did. Many are curious about his motives for doing this to himself. Some Blacks are angry, accusing him of no longer wanting to be Black—a sentiment attributed by the writers of *Saturday Night Live* to the fictional Queen Shenequa. Others worry about the kind of message he is sending to his youngest fans: more powerfully than words ever could, isn't his surgical transformation telling Black children that if they have dark skin, large lips, Negroid features, and nappy hair, they are not beautiful?

On the other hand, many Blacks who criticize Michael Jackson may themselves straighten their hair with perms or curl activators, lighten their skin with fade creams, or try to alter the shape of their noses with clothespins, makeup, or surgery. What Jackson has done to himself is no more than what many others might do, given the money and the opportunity. Michael Jackson did not invent Black self-hatred. He is simply the product of an environment with a long history of race and color bias.

More recently, Jackson appears to be exploring his African heritage. In the opinion of Teddy Riley, the creator of "New Jack Swing" and the producer of Jackson's *Black or White* album, Jackson regrets what he has done. In an article in *Rolling Stone,* journalist Michael Goldberg quotes Riley as saying that if Jackson had it to do all over again, he "would not have done that." Riley adds that "once you change your description, you can't turn back. You can't get your own face or your own skin back again. But he is still Michael Jackson; he is still the talented man that everyone grew up on.'' Goldberg perhaps sums it up best when he writes that Jackson ''is an extraordinarily talented man with a gift for creating music that people all over the world love. Jackson should put more faith in his talent. That, more than anything, accounts for his more than twenty years of stardom.''

Images of Blacks in the media reflect how much progress has been made, and how much still needs to be made, in the area of race relations and color consciousness. While Black heroines in novels no longer have to die tragically for the sake of a moral lesson about the dangers of race mixing, and Black actors no longer have to be cast as buffoons to get stage or film parts, certain color stereotypes persist. Casting for films and music videos still follows traditional color patterns, with a Black female romantic interest always lighter than her Black lover. Yet even in this media-driven culture of ours there is room for hope. Alice Walker and Spike Lee are high-powered figures in literature and film, respectively, and both have done much to open doors for other Blacks in their media. As more and more African-American writers, directors, songwriters, artists, and journalists are able to free themselves from the influence of institutionalized racism in their various media, an increasing number will openly explore the psychology of race and color.

Epilogue:
About Change

The world belongs to the strong
regardless of a little pigmentation more or less.
—ZORA NEALE HURSTON

This book is not the final word on intraracial skin-color discrimination, nor was it ever meant to be. Some readers will be disappointed to find that a particular slant on the subject has not been covered, but it would have been impossible to capture every perspective on such a volatile issue. What we have attempted to do is to create the framework for an understanding of why issues of skin color, hair, and features remain so important to African Americans today.

Some may accuse us of "airing dirty laundry." From the point of view of those who believe that certain matters are better left unspoken, perhaps we have. Others may legitimately be concerned that if Whites know about the color prejudice inside the Black community, they will take complaints of White racism less seriously. Predictably, some Whites will declare, "If Blacks can't take care of their own problems with discrimination, how can they expect us to do any better?" While not denying that such a reaction is possible, we maintain that the potential for consciousness raising far outweighs any risk of a racist backlash. Besides, those who truly understand intraracial color discrimination will realize that it is deeply rooted in societal racism.

A growing cadre of artists, authors, and performers in the Black community are confronting color consciousness through their creative endeavors. From a variety of perspectives, they are sharing with others their experiences with color discrimination—and with each step toward openness comes greater understanding. A surprising number of Whites, for example, have said that Spike Lee's 1988 film, *School Daze*, was their first exposure to the issue of color discrimination within the Black community.

Several contemporary Black authors are addressing concerns about color in their works, including Toni Morrison in *The Bluest Eye* (1970) and *Tar Baby* (1981), Audre Lorde in *Sister Outsider* (1984), and Maya Angelou in *I Know Why the Caged Bird Sings* (1979). Alice Walker, the author of the highly acclaimed *The Color Purple* (1982), is credited with coining the term "colorism" in an essay she wrote for *Essence* in 1982. Lisa Jones of the *Village Voice* regularly examines the politics of skin color and hairstyle in her columns, and author Bonita Porter recently published a novel called *Colorstruck*.

Comedian and actress Whoopi Goldberg is another who has exposed Black women's private feelings of inadequacy about their color and hair. In one skit, first performed during the eighties, Goldberg pretends to be a little girl depressed about her short, nappy hair, her dark skin, and her brown eyes. Solace comes when she drapes a white blouse over her head and discovers that it magically transforms her into a little White girl with beautiful long blond hair that can be flipped and flung about. While hilariously funny, the skit also makes a poignant statement about the impossibility of trying to adhere to a White standard of attractiveness when one is Black.

The Black playwright George C. Wolfe, in *The Colored Museum* (1990), similarly uses humor to challenge attitudes about hair. In one scene, two wigs on a dressing table are talking to a bald Black woman, each trying to convince her that *it* is the wig she should wear when she gives her boyfriend the ax. LaWanda, a long flowing wig, emphasizes the powerful effect of being able to toss her hair back with emotion, and the other wig, an Afro named Janine, reminds her of the virtues and strength of hair that is natural. Theatergoers admit that *The Colored Museum* induces feelings of both joy and pain, to which Wolfe replies, "Wounds heal better in open air. . . . We've landed people on the moon, and Black folks are still talking about 'good hair.' "

Barbara Brandon, the nation's first syndicated Black female cartoonist, draws a strip called "Where I'm Coming From" populated by a group of Black women friends among whom the subjects of skin color and hair often arise.

Even a film director from India, Mira Nair, has explored the psychology of color in her 1992 release, *Mississippi Masala*. The plot centers on the interracial relationship of a Black man (Denzel Washington) and his dark-skinned Indian girlfriend, Mina, who has lived in Mississippi with her parents since their expulsion from Uganda during the 1960s rule of Idi Amin. The film, which makes several references to Mina's dark color, may surprise many viewers by its revelation that the color complexes endemic to the African-American community affect Indians as well.

While it is encouraging to see so many African Americans breaking the silence on this old issue, some may ask, "What difference does skin color make in light of the high rates of Black-on-Black crime, issues of police brutality, teenage pregnancy, high-school dropouts, Black unemployment, drug addiction, and AIDS in the Black community?" Certainly color discrimination lacks the urgency of any of these other social ills, yet each problem has roots in economic disadvantage (which disproportionately affects those who are dark skinned) and is also related to low self-esteem. The inability to accept oneself, whether because of skin color or for some other reason, spawns a disrespect for and intolerance of others. In some urban areas, Black children who do well in school are accused by their peers of "acting White." Those who also happen to "look White" because of lighter skin color are also targeted for ridicule. To maintain their popularity, some of these children start failing on purpose, behavior that in turn contributes to high dropout rates, unemployment, poverty, and, ultimately, violence.

Color discrimination is multifaceted, with deep roots in our nation's history, and therefore is not subject to a quick fix. Yet there are a few basic things that Blacks—and Whites as well—can do to minimize the damage that colorism will inflict on future generations. First, the topic of intraracial color discrimination must be brought out of the closet. Despite what some may claim, this hurtful issue has not gone away. Second, more research is needed to document the effects of the problem on the African-American community. A greater understanding of the historical, social, and legal implications of the one-drop rule would also help. Third, White personnel managers, therapists, teachers, doctors, and others should be better informed about color prejudice, through seminars and documentaries like Kathe Sandler's *A Question of Color*. Many Whites in positions of authority remain ignorant of and insensitive to the role of color in the lives of African Americans. Fourth, Black parents need to alert their children to color bias and teach them how to respond to it. Fifth, on an individual level, Americans of all races must work together to overcome stereotypes about color, including the assumptions that dark-skinned Black men are more criminally dangerous and that light-skinned Black women are more feminine and beautiful. Therapy may be helpful to those who cannot work through on their own the anger and depression they feel about their own color complex.

We offer this book in the hope that it will help to heal some of the wounds the color issue has inflicted on the African-American community. The first step is awareness.

Sources

For each chapter, these source notes cite both specific and general references, listed in the order in which the material appears in the text.

Introduction

1. Opening quotation by Mabel Lincoln in John L. Gwaltney, *Drylongso: A Self-Portrait of Black America* (New York: Random House, 1980), p. 66.
2. Drew angrily addressing Flipper in a pivotal fight scene in *Jungle Fever*, dir. Spike Lee, Universal Pictures, 1991.

1: Masters, Slaves and Lovers

1. "Jamaica, a Poem in Three Parts," in W. D. Jordan, *White over Black: American Attitudes Toward the Negro, 1550–1812* (Chapel Hill: University of North Carolina Press, 1968), p. 150.
2. Reference to English settlers raping and impregnating Indian women in Sara M. Evans, *Born for Liberty* (New York: Free Press, 1989), pp. 12–14.
3. Reference to slaves being brought from Santo Domingo in Malcolm Cowley and Daniel P. Mannix, "Middle Passage," *American Heritage,* vol. 13, no. 2 (1962), p. 22.
4. Reference to colonial Blacks who lived free in Nathan I. Huggins, *Black Odyssey: The African American Ordeal in Slavery* (New York: Vintage Books, 1990), p. 13.
5. Discussion of the legality of slavery in colonial America in G. T. Hull, P. B. Scott, and B. Smith, eds., *But Some of Us Are Brave* (Old Westbury, N.Y.: Feminist Press, 1982), p. 72.
6. Reference to the raping of female slaves by White sailors in Huggins, *Black Odyssey,* p. 43.
7. Reference to percent of English immigrants who were indentured servants in Suzanne Lebsock, "No Obey," in Nancy A. Hewitt, *Women, Families, and Communities: Readings in American History,* vol. 1, *To 1877* (Glenview, Ill.: Foresman/Little, Brown Higher Education, 1990), p. 12.
8. Reference to relationships between indentured servants and Black slaves in Joel Williamson, *New People: Miscegenation and Mulattoes in the United States* (New York: Free Press, 1980), pp. 6–14.
9. Reference to race mixing in early America in Lebsock, p. 12.
10. Reference to interracial marriages in Lebsock, p. 15.
11. Account of 1622 massacre and Indians referring to Black men as "Manitto" in Lerone Bennett, Jr., *The Shaping of Black America* (Chicago: Johnson Publishing Co., 1975), pp. 87–88.

167

12. Reference to whole tribes of Indians absorbed into Black population in Gunnar Myrdal, *An American Dilemma* (New York: Harper & Row, 1944), p. 124.

13. Reference to colonial race mixing in today's Blacks in F. James Davis, *Who Is Black?: One Nation's Definition* (University Park: Pennsylvania State University Press, 1991), p. 21.

14. Reference to Virginia Massacre in Bennett, *The Shaping of Black America,* p. 88.

15. Reference to love relationships among slaves and Indians in Huggins, *Black Odyssey,* p. 209.

16. Antimiscegenation laws discussed in Davis, *Who Is Black,* p. 33.

17. Protest by Richard Tilghman in Hull, Scott, and Smith, *But Some of Us Are Brave,* pp. 88 – 89.

18. White owners encouraging rape of servants in Huggins, *Black Odyssey,* p. xli.

19. Law of 1662 concerning status of children in Williamson, *New People,* p. 8.

20. Discussion of Black children who were considered free depending on status of their parents in E. Franklin Frazier, *The Negro in the United States* (New York: Alfred A. Knopf, 1957), p. 26.

21. Discussion of legal issues concerning one ounce of Black blood in Davis, *Who Is Black?,* p. 34.

22. Discussion of mulattoes passing as Whites in Davis, *Who Is Black?,* p. 34.

23. Reference to three-tiered social system in the lower South in Davis, p. 35.

24. Reference to owners freeing slaves when America declared its independence in Evans, *Born for Liberty,* pp. 52 – 53.

25. Discussion of the free colored in Carole Ione, *Pride of Family* (New York: Summit Books, 1991), p. 128.

26. Discussion of color-conscious Creoles and their rise to power in Davis, *Who Is Black?,* pp. 34 – 36.

27. Quotation by newly freed slave in New Orleans in Charles Johnson, *Middle Passage* (New York: Atheneum, 1990), p. 9.

28. Reference to three-tiered racial classification preferred by Creoles in Virginia R. Dominquez, *White by Definition: Social Classification in Creole Louisiana* (New Brunswick, N.J.: Rutgers University Press, 1986), pp. 163 – 64.

29. Discussion of skin color and privilege in Bart Landry, *The New Black Middle Class* (Berkeley and Los Angeles: University of California Press, 1987), pp. 24–25.

30. Reference to mulattoes in the South remaining enslaved before 1860 in Williamson, *New People,* pp. 24–33.

31. Reference to mulattoes being worth more on slave market in Myrdal, *An American Dilemma,* p. 696.

32. Reference to friction among slaves due to skin tone differences in Frazier, *The Negro in the United States,* p. 274, and Na'im Akbar, *Chains and Images of Psychological Slavery* (Jersey City, N.J.: New Mind Production, 1984), p. 24.

33. Discussion of rape and molestation of young slave girls in Davis, *Who Is Black,* p. 34, and G. Lerner, *Black Women in White America: A Documentary History* (New York: Vintage Books, 1972), pp. 158 – 59.

34. Reference to White men fantasizing about Black slave women in Huggins, *Black Odyssey*, p. 144.
35. Discussion of breeding mulatto women for profit in Davis, *Who Is Black*, p. 38.
36. Case of William Adams in Judith K. Shafer, "Open and Notorious Concubinage: The Emancipation of Slave Mistresses by Will and the Supreme Court in Antebellum Louisiana," *Louisiana History*, vol. 28, 1987, pp. 165–82.
37. Case of Thomas Jefferson's affair with slave woman discussed in Williamson, *New People*, pp. 43–47, and Irma Hunt, *Dearest Madame: The President's Mistresses* (New York: McGraw-Hill, 1978), pp. 51–71.
38. Reference to sexual exploitation of all female slaves in Williamson, p. 42, and Hunt, *Dearest Madame*, p. 40.
39. Reference to White wives punishing house servants in Huggins, *Black Odyssey*, p. 145.
40. Excerpt of White wife abusing servant in Margaret Walker, *Jubilee* (New York: Bantam Books, 1966), p. 26.
41. Quotation on White wife's harsh treatment of Black slave girl who wanted to get married in Harriet Jacob, *Incidents in the Life of a Slave Girl* (Coral Gables, Fla.: Mnemosyne Publishing Co., 1969), p. 59.
42. Reference to White women who accepted sexual relations between their husbands and slave girls in Lerner, *Black Women in White America*, pp. 158–59.
43. Examples of male slaves seducing their owners' wives and daughters in Mary Berry and John Blassingame, *Long Memory: The Black Experience in America* (New York: Oxford University Press, 1982), p. 119.
44. Opinions for White woman who gave birth to mulatto baby in Davis, *Who Is Black?*, p. 62.
45. Discussion of repercussions for Black men sexually involved with White women in Calvin Hernton, *Sex and Racism in America* (New York: Grove, 1965), p. 19, and F. G. Wood, *Black Scare* (Los Angeles: University of California Press, 1968).
46. Discussion of one-drop rule in Davis, *Who Is Black*, pp. 35, 49.
47. Reference to decline of social and sexual relations between Whites and Blacks after Civil War in Davis, pp. 41, 49.
48. Reference to Angolan Blacks in Davis, p. 21.

2: The Color Gap in Power and Privilege

1. Opening quotation of Blue Vein societies' fictional creed in Wallace Thurman, *The Blacker the Berry* (New York: Macmillan Publishing Co., 1970, originally published London: Macaulay Publishing, 1929), p. 21.
2. Origins of Blue Vein societies in E. Franklin Frazier, *The Black Bourgeois* (New York: Collier, 1962); discussion of Blue Vein societies also in Joel Williamson, *New People: Miscegenation and Mulattoes in the United States* (New York: Free Press, 1980), p. 82.
3. Discussion of Strivers Row in Williamson, *New People*, pp. 162–63, Stephen Birmingham, *Certain People* (Boston: Little, Brown and Company, 1977), pp.

183–193, and Jervis Anderson, *This Was Harlem* (New York: Farrar, Straus & Giroux, 1982), pp. 339–40.

4. Quote by Adam Clayton Powell, Sr., on Strivers Row in Anderson, *This Was Harlem*, p. 340.

5. Reference to Sugar Hill in Anderson, p. 340.

6. Reference about 409 Edgecomb from telephone interview, Nov. 1990.

7. Reference to DuBois calling church "the social center of Negro life" in Willard B. Gatewood, *Aristocrats of Color: The Black Elite, 1880–1920* (Bloomington and Indianapolis: Indiana University Press, 1990), p. 272.

8. Discussion of CME and DuBois's quote in Gatewood, *Aristocrats of Color*, p. 152.

9. Reference to First Congregational Church in Atlanta in Birmingham, *Certain People*, p. 225.

10. Description of paper-bag test in John Langston Gwaltney, *Drylongso* (New York: Random House, 1980), p. 80.

11. Discussion of comb test in Margo Okazawa-Rey, Tracy Robinson, and Janie V. Ward, "Black Women and the Politics of Skin Color and Hair," *Women's Study Quarterly,* vol. 14, nos. 1, 2 (1986), pp. 13–14, and Charles Parrish, "The Significance of Color in the Negro Community," unpublished doctoral dissertation, University of Chicago, 1944, and Dominguez, *White by Definition* p. 164.

12. Discussions of color and higher education in Sidney Kronus, *The Black Middle Class* (Columbus, Ohio: Merrill Publishers, 1971), p. 71, and Myrdal, *An American Dilemma,* p. 694.

13. Discussion of Palmer Institute in Birmingham, *Certain People*, pp. 1–8.

14. Discussion of Dunbar school in Gatewood, *Aristocrats of Color*, p. 263.

15. Reference to 1916 statistics on students in several Black institutions in Alexander H. Shannon, *The Racial Integrity of the American Negro* (Nashville, Tenn.: Parthenon Press, 1951), p. 45.

16. Discussion of Tuskegee Institute in Shannon, *The Racial Integrity of the American Negro,* p. 45.

17. Reference to Daytona School (later Bethune-Cookman College) being for "Black" girls, not fair-skinned girls, in Birmingham, *Certain People*, p. 285.

18. Reference to Moten becoming president of Tuskegee in Shannon, *The Racial Integrity of the American Negro,* p. 45.

19. Research on skin color and career aspirations in Ronald E. Hall, "The Projected Manifestations of Aspiration, Personal Values, and Environmental Assessment Cognates of Cutaneo-chroma (Skin-Color) for a Selected Population of African Americans," unpublished doctoral dissertation, Atlanta University, July 1989.

20. Reference to fraternity color-tax parties in C. Eric Lincoln, "Color and Group Identity in the United States," *Daedulus,* vol. 96 (1967), pp. 527–41.

21. Discussion of Brown Fellowship Society in Gatewood, *Aristocrats of Color*, pp. 14, 156.

22. Discussion of DuBois's Talented Tenth list in Edward Reuter, *The Mulatto in the United States* (New York: Haskell House Publishers, 1969), and John H.

Franklin and August Meier, *Black Leaders of the Twentieth Century* (Chicago: University of Illinois Press, 1982), pp. 63–70.

23. Reference to Washington and DuBois having light skin in Davis, *Who Is Black,* pp. 5–7.

24. Reference to Frederick Douglass in Wilson J. Moses, review of *Frederick Douglass,* by William S. McFeely, *Washington Post,* Jan. 20, 1991.

25. Reference to Purvis in Davis, *Who Is Black?,* p. 6.

26. Reference to James Augustine Healy as "second founder" of Georgetown University in Davis, *Who Is Black: One Nation's Definition* (University Park: Pennsylvania State University Press, 1991), p. 7.

27. Reference to number of Black congressmen and senators during Reconstruction in Shannon, *The Racial Integrity of the American Negro,* p. 42, and Davis, *Who Is Black,* p. 6.

28. Reference to fact that not all Black leaders were light skinned in Robert Staples, *Introduction to Black Sociology* (New York: McGraw-Hill, 1976), p. 310.

29. Reference to Jonathan Wright in Williamson, *New People,* p. 87.

30. Reference to Beverly Nash in E. L. Thornbrough, *Black Reconstructionist* (Englewood Cliffs, N.J.: Prentice-Hall, 1972), p. 51.

31. Discussion of William Whipper in Carole Ione, *Pride of Family* (New York: Simon & Schuster, 1991), pp. 170–71.

32. Discussion of Marcus Garvey as apostle of pure Blackness in Williamson, *New People,* p. 159.

33. Reference to DuBois trying to "be everything else but a Negro" in Gatewood, *Aristocrats of Color,* p. 321.

34. Discussion of conflict between DuBois and Garvey in Franklin and Meier, *Black Leaders of the Twentieth Century,* pp. 76–83.

35. Description of Garvey as uplifting the spirits of dark-skinned Blacks in Williamson, *New People,* pp. 160–61.

36. Reference to the Reverend Adam Clayton Powell, Jr., in Davis, *Who Is Black?,* p. 2.

37. Description of Walter White as one sixty-fourth Black in Davis, p. 56.

38. Discussions of A. Philip Randolph and Martin Luther King, Jr., in Davis, pp. 7–8.

39. Extensive discussion of one-drop rule in Davis, pp. 1–187.

40. Bonnie Allen quotation in her "It Ain't Easy Being Pinky," *Essence,* July 1982, pp. 67–68, 127–28.

41. Discussion of sixties upheaval and color in telephone interview with Lillie Edwards, associate professor of history, DePaul University, on Jan 29, 1991.

42. Research on measurement of facial features in Melville Herkovits, *The American Negro* (Bloomington: Indiana University Press, 1968), p. 61.

43. Research on ratio of earnings of light-skinned and dark-skinned Blacks in Michael G. Hughes and Bradley R. Hertel, "The Significance of Color Remains: A Study of Life Chances, Mate Selection, and Ethnic Consciousness Among Black Americans," *Social Forces,* vol. 68, no. 4 (1990), pp. 1–16.

44. Research on color and success in Veran M. Keith and Cedric Herring, "Skin

Tone and Stratification in the Black Community,'' *American Journal of Sociology,* vol. 97, no. 3 (1991), pp. 760–78.

45. Reference to Willie Horton in Martin Schram, "The Making of Willie Horton," *New Republic,* May 1990, pp. 17–19.
46. Reference to Sharon Pratt (Dixon) Kelly in Mary Ann French, "Who Is Sharon Pratt Dixon?," *Jet,* April 1991, pp. 54–56.

3: Embracing Whiteness

1. Opening quote in Maya Angelou, *I Know Why the Caged Bird Sings* (New York: Bantam Books, 1969), p. 2.
2. Quote about Emma Lou's unfortunate coloring in Wallace Thurman, *The Blacker the Berry* (New York: Macmillan Publishing Co., 1929), p. 4.
3. Quote about Claudia's Aryan-looking doll in Toni Morrison, *The Bluest Eye* (New York: Holt, 1970), p. 22.
4. Reference to Black girls' feelings of shame in William Grier and Price M. Cobbs, *Black Rage* (New York: Basic Books, 1968), pp. 42–43.
5. Discussion of adoption practices in Birmingham, *Certain People,* p. 161.
6. Discussion of Mme. C. J. Walker in A'Lelia P. Bundles, "Madam C. J. Walker: Cosmetics Tycoon," *Ms.,* July 1983, pp. 91–94, and A'Lelia P. Bundles, *Madam C. J. Walker: Entrepreneur* (New York: Chelsea House Publishers, 1991), telephone interview with A'Lelia P. Bundles in May 1992 and the film *Two Dollars and a Dream,* dir. Stanley Nelson, distr. Filmmakers Library, 124 E. 40th St., New York, N.Y. 10016, 1988.
7. Lyrics of "Nappy Headed Blues" from *Two Dollars and a Dream.*
8. Analysis of ads for hair products in Bertice Barry, "Black-on-Black Discrimination: The Phenomenon of Colorism Among African Americans," unpublished doctoral research, Sociology Department, Kent State University, Kent, Ohio, 1988.
9. Discussion of hairstyles originating in Africa in Naomi Sims, *All About Black Health and Beauty for the Black Woman* (Garden City, N.Y.: Doubleday, 1976), pp. 69–76.
10. Discussion of contact lenses in Elsie B. Washington, "The Bluest Eyes," *Essence,* Jan. 1988, p. 114.
11. Discussion of blue-eyed Black woman on magazine cover in Bonnie Allen, "It Ain't Easy Being Pinky," *Essence,* July 1982, p. 67.
12. Reference to use of lemon juice and bleach to lighten skin in Angela Neal and Midge Wilson, "The Role of Skin Color and Features in the Black Community: Implications for Black Women and Therapy," *Clinical Psychology Review,* vol. 9 (1989), p. 329.
13. Discussion of bleach bath in Abraham Kardiner and Lionel Oversey, *The Mark of Oppression* (New York: World, 1951).
14. Statement by Dr. Yusaboro Noguchi in *The Literary Digest,* Nov. 23, 1929.
15. Reference to how much money is spent on skin-bleaching products in "A Study in Hype and Risk: The Marketing of Skin Bleaches," a report by the City of

New York Dept. of Consumer Affairs, Mark Green, Commissioner, Feb. 1992, p. 1.

16. Reference about discovery of hydroquinone in "Real Truth About Skin Whiteners," *Ebony*, Jan. 1950, pp. 15–18.

17. Reference to HQ safety concerns in "A Study in Hype and Risk: The Marketing of Skin Bleaches," a report by the City of New York Dept. of Consumer Affairs, Feb. 1992.

18. Reference to LaToya Jackson's claim that her brother Michael has lupus in Tananarive Due, "Skin Deep," *Miami Herald*, Oct. 2, 1991.

19. Description of dermabrasion process in "Repairing the Damage," *Self*, Oct. 1989, p. 142.

20. Dr. Robert Auerbach's comments on dermabrasion in "Repairing the Damage," p. 142.

21. Barbara Walden's comments on *Sonya Live in L.A.*, Cable News Network, Jan. 31, 1990.

22. Discussion of tanning in Susan Brownmiller, *Femininity* (New York: Fawcett Columbine, 1984).

23. Discussion of "white is righter" theory in Pierre Van den Berge and Peter Frost, "Skin Color Preference, Sexual Dimorphism, and Sexual Selection: A Case of Gene Culture Co-evolution?," *Ethnic and Racial Studies*, vol. 9 (1986), pp. 87–113.

24. Reference to Brazil's demographics in Charles Whitaker, "Blacks in Brazil," *Ebony*, Feb. 1991, pp. 58–64, 107.

25. Telephone interview with Alice Windom on June 2, 1991.

26. Discussion of color confrontation theory in Dr. Frances Cress Welsing, *The Isis Papers: The Keys to the Colors* (Chicago: Third World Press, 1991).

27. Mention of Aztec women smearing yellowish ointment on their faces in Van den Berge and Frost, "Skin Color Preference, Sexual Dimorphism, and Sexual Selection."

28. Japanese proverb and mention of Lady Murasaki's *Tale of Genji* in Hiroshi Wagatsuma's "The Social Perception of Skin Color in Japan" in J. H. Franklin, *Color and Race* (Boston: Houghton Mifflin, 1968), pp. 129–30.

29. Mention of caste and color in Franklin, *Color and Race*, p. xii.

30. Reference to Moroccan proverb in Franklin, p. 192.

31. Reference to Arab countries' admiration for girls as white as snow in Van den Berge and Frost, "Skin Color Preference, Seuxal Dimorphism, and Seuxal Selection."

32. Discussion of art and color in Brownmiller, *Femininity*, p. 132.

33. Mention of anthropological listing and Darwin's sex-linked theory regarding skin color in Van den Berge and Frost, "Skin Color Preference, Sexual Dimorphism, and Sexual Selection."

34. Discussion of neotenous hypothesis in Van den Berge and Frost.

35. Discussion of skin color and fecundability in Van den Berge and Frost.

36. Importance of skin color in different cultures discussed in Franklin, *Color and Race*, p. 268.

37. Quote by Roger Bastide in Franklin, p. 37.

38. Discussion of color symbolism in Kenneth J. Gergen, "The Significance of Skin Color in Human Relations," in Franklin, *Color and Race,* pp. 390–406.
39. Reference to *Webster's Third New International Dictionary* definitions of black and white in August Wilson, "I Don't Want to Hire Nobody, Just 'Cause They're Black," *Spin,* Oct. 1990, pp. 70–71.
40. Truman speaking on color symbolism in Thurman, *The Blacker the Berry,* p. 144.
41. Discussion of South African color system in *The South Africa Fact Sheet,* New York Africa Fund, 1988.
42. Comments by Winnie Mandela on *Phil Donahue Show,* NBC, June 25, 1990.

4: Black Identity: Shades of Beauty and Pride

1. Discussion of cognitive concept of constancy in M. A. Spencer, G. K. Brookins, and W. R. Allen, *Beginnings: The Social and Affective Development of Black Children* (Hillside, N.J.: Lawrence Erlbaum Associates, 1985), p. 181.
2. Comment on Black children achieving concept of constancy in Spencer, Brookins, and Allen, *Beginnings,* p. 181.
3. Discussion of doll tests in K. B. and M. B. Clark, "Racial Identification of Negro Preschool Children," in *Readings in Social Psychology* (New York: Maccoby, Newcomb, and Hartley, Holt-Rinehart, 1947).
4. Excerpt from Richard Kluger, *Simple Justice: The History of Brown v. Board of Education* (NY: Alfred A. Knopf, 1976), quoted in Michele Wallace, *Invisibility Blues: From Pop to Theory* (New York: Verso, 1990), p. 170.
5. Discussion of methodological criticism of doll tests in J. A. Baldwin, "Theory and Research Concerning the Notion of Black Self-hatred: A Review and Reinterpretation," *Journal of Black Psychology,* vol. 5 (1979), pp. 51–77.
6. Subsequent retesting of Black children's doll preferences in Michael Barnes, "Colorism: In American Society," *Los Angeles Times,* April 24, 1988.
7. Additional experiments on doll preferences of Black children in Darlene Powell-Hobson and Derek S. Hobson, *Journal of Black Psychology,* vol. 14 (1988), pp. 57–63.
8. Reference to Mattel dolls in "A Celebration of Black Identity Toys," *Ebony,* Dec. 1991, pp. 23–24.
9. Description of Kenya doll from Tyco Industries in *Chicago Tribune* (Feb. 23, 1992), Woman News, sec. 6, p. 6.
10. Discussion of Black children's rare use of skin color for racial grouping in M. N. Alejandro-Wright, "The Child's Conception of Racial Classification: A Socio-cognitive Developmental Model," in Spencer, Brookins, and Allen, *Beginnings,* p. 186.
11. Discussion of emerging sensitivity about skin-color differences in M. B. Spencer and C. Marstrom-Adams, "Identity Processes Among Racial and Ethnic Minority Children in America," *Child Development,* vol. 61, 1990, pp. 290–310.
12. Mention of skin color and errors in racial identification in George Gitter, David Mostofsky, and Yoichi Satow, "The Effect of Skin Color and Physiognomy on

Racial Misidentification," *Journal of Social Psychology,* vol. 88, 1972, pp. 139–143.

13. Personal interview with Katie K. on Jan. 16, 1992.

14. Discussion of stereotypes about skin color in Charles Parrish, "Color Names and Color Notions," *Journal of Negro Education,* vol. 15 (1946), pp. 13–20.

15. Plight of Jeffrey described in Itabari Njeri, "Who Is Black?," *Essence,* Sept. 1991, pp. 64–66, 114–16.

16. Discussion of plight of light-skinned men in Michel Marriott, "Light Skinned Men: Problems and Privileges," *Essence,* Nov. 1988, p. 76.

17. Personal interview with Ron Holt in January 1992.

18. Unpublished laboratory research by Dr. Midge Wilson conducted in 1991–92 at DePaul University, Chicago.

19. Discussion of girls' sensitivity to skin color in Cornelia Porter, "Social Reasons for Skin Tone Preferences of Black School-Age Children," *American Journal of Orthopsychiatry,* Jan. 1991, pp. 149–54.

20. Personal interview with Maisha Bennett in February 1991.

21. Studies on skin tone and self-satisfaction or dissatisfaction in Janie Ward and Tracy Robinson, "Perception of Physical Attractiveness for Black Adolescents," paper presented at 97th American Psychological Association convention, New Orleans, La., August 1989.

22. Reference to self-esteem of Black versus White girls in E. L. Horwitz, "Short-changing Girls, Shortchanging America," *Outlook,* vol. 85, no. 2 (April/May 1991), pp. 16–20.

23. Research by Selena Bond and Thomas F. Cash in "Black Beauty: Skin Color and Body Images among African-American College Women," *Journal of Applied Social Psychology,* vol. 22 (1992), pp. 874–88.

24. Personal interview with Carolyn in January 1992.

25. Assignment of stereotypically Black names to dark-skinned unattractive women in unpublished laboratory research by Dr. Midge Wilson conducted in 1991–92 at DePaul University.

26. Personal interview with Carolyn in January 1992.

27. Reference to Black Americans forsaking their slave names in Itabari Njeri, *Every Good-bye Ain't Gone* (New York: Times Books/Random House, 1982), pp. 224–25.

28. Personal interview with Jaleel Abdul-Adil on Jan. 29, 1992.

29. Discussion of race designators in L. Roberts, "Identity Crisis," *Upscale,* June/July 1991, pp. 52–53.

30. Personal interview with Eric F. on Dec. 27, 1991.

31. Discussion of deracination in Vincent D. Colbert, "The Effects of Racial Isolation on a Female Black Middle-Class Population: Does It Lead to Deracination?," unpublished master's thesis, DePaul University, Chicago, 1988.

32. Quote by Joan Morgan, "The Family Trap," *Essence,* Sept. 1990, p. 81.

33. Reference to oreos, coconuts, bananas, and apples in Ronald Hall, "The Bleaching Syndrome," unpublished manuscript.

34. Suggestions for light-skinned Blacks on handling their conflicts in F. James

Davis, *Who Is Black: One Nation's Definition* (University Park: Pennsylvania State University Press, 1991), pp. 149–50.

35. Quote by Kathleen Cross in her "Trapped in the Body of a White Woman," *Ebony*, Oct. 1990, p. 74.

36. General advantages of one-drop rule discussed in Davis, *Who Is Black?*.

37. Reference to Charles Stewart's remarks in Njeri, "Who Is Black," pp. 64, 66, 115–16.

38. Quote by playwright Velina Hasu Houston on "Mom's White, Dad's Black: I Will Choose My Own Race," *Phil Donahue Show* (NBC), Nov. 19, 1991.

39. Telephone interview with Ramona Douglass in January 1992.

40. Telephone interview with Carlos Fernandez in January 1992.

41. Discussion of 1990 census figures on 9.8 million checking "other" in Felicity Barringer, "Census Bureau Shows Profound Change in Racial Makeup," *New York Times*, Mar. 11, 1991, B8.

42. Telephone interview with Dr. Barbara Love in January 1992.

43. Comments by Jasmine Guy in "Are the Children of Mixed Marriages Black or White?," *Jet*, May 21, 1990, pp. 52–54.

44. Comment by Jennifer Beals in "Are the Children of Mixed Marriages Black or White?"

45. Personal interview with Renee Tenison in May 1990

46. Comment by Paula Abdul in Lynn Norment, "Who's Black and Who's Not?," *Ebony*, Mar. 1990, pp. 134, 136, 138.

47. Discussion of Phipps case in Davis, *Who Is Black?*, pp. 7–8.

48. Comment by Gene Lees in his "John, Gil, Dave and the Man on the Buffalo Nickel," *Jazzletter*, vol. 10, no. 9 (Sept. 1990), p. 3.

49. Discussion of personal conflict when physical features do not match inner self in P. M. Brown, "Biracial Identity and Social Marginality," *Child and Adolescent Social Work*, vol. 7 (1990), pp. 319–37.

5: Hair: The Straight and Nappy of It All

1. Opening quotation by A'Lelia Perry Bundles from telephone interview in May 1992.

2. Discussion of femininity of hair in Susan Brownmiller, *Femininity* (New York: Fawcett Columbine, 1984), p. 76.

3. Excerpt by Gerald Early in "Life with Daughters or The Cakewalk with Shirley Temple," *The Hungry Mind Review*, Vol. 20 (Winter 1991–92), pp. 6–9.

4. Description of trip to Virgin Gorda in Audre Lorde, "Is Your Hair Still Political?," *Essence*, Sept. 1990, p. 40.

5. Poem by Gwendolyn Brooks, "To Those of My Sisters Who Kept Their Naturals," *Primer for Blacks* (Chicago: Third World Press, 1991).

6. Comment by actress Whoopi Goldberg on *Arsenio Hall Show*, CBS, Dec. 11, 1990.

7. Comment by actress Cicely Tyson on *Arsenio Hall Show*, Dec. 12, 1990.

8. Naadu Blankson's discussion of hair in her "The Dreaded Decision," *Essence*, Oct. 1990, Interior sec., p. 36.

9. Comment by Alice Walker about dreadlocking in a letter she wrote to *Essence,* Oct. 1990, p. 36.
10. Personal interview with Simone Hylton in January 1992.
11. Nantil Chardonnay's comment on Bo Derek's braids in her "Braids: Cultural Connection," *BE,* vol. 45 (Feb./Mar. 1991), pp. 44–72.
12. Dialogue from *School Daze* in Spike Lee and L. Jones, *Uplift the Race: The Construction of School Daze* (New York: Simon & Schuster, 1988) pp. 154–57.
13. Halle Berry's comments on hair in Elsie B. Washington, "Beauty and Health," *Hair Attitudes,* Jan. 1992, pp. 68–69.

6: Divided Families and Friends

1. Opening quote in Anne Rice, *The Feast of All Saints* (New York: Ballantine, 1979), p. 486.
2. Reference to Black families' stresses over skin color in Nancy Boyd-Franklin, *Black Families in Therapy: A Multisystems Approach* (New York: Guilford Press, 1989), pp. 34–41.
3. Mention of Malcolm X and Elliot Liebow in S. Bond and T. Cash, "Black Beauty: Skin Color and Body Image among African-American College Women."
4. Personal interview with Sandra Braine in July 1991
5. Discussion of Dr. Lightfoot's mother in Sara Lawrence Lightfoot, *Balm in Gilead: Journey of a Healer* (Reading, Pa.: Addison-Wesley, 1988), pp. 114–16.
6. Quote about mother applying straighteners in Joan Morgan, "The Family Trap," *Essence,* Sept. 1990, p. 82.
7. Quote by Nettie Jones, *The Mischief Makers* (New York: Weidenfeld & Nicholson, 1989), p. 4.
8. Eartha Kitt's story from interview on *60 Minutes,* CBS, Aug. 12, 1990.
9. Discussion of foster placement in S. Daley, "Foster Placement by Skin Tone Seen," *New York Times,* Jan. 17, 1990, B1, B3.
10. Telephone interview with Sydney Duncan in October 1991.
11. Reference to adoption practices of some wealthy black families in Stephen Birmingham, *Certain People* (Boston: Little, Brown, 1977), p. 161.
12. Reference to NABSW's stand on interracial adoptions in Karen Grigsby Bates, "Are You My Mother?," *Essence,* April 1991, p. 50.
13. Story about Lena Horne's childhood in *In Person* (New York: Greenberg Publisher, 1950).
14. Dialogue between Keyonn and Keith from *A Question of Color,* dir. Kathe Sandler, PBS, 1992.
15. Quotes from *Teen Summit* show, Black Entertainment Television, Nov. 3, 1990.
16. Quote about Black girls being misfits in Michele Wallace, *Invisibility Blues: From Pop to Theory* (New York: Verso, 1990), p. 21.
17. Letter to "Ebony Advisor" in *Ebony,* May 1990, p. 116.

7: Dating and Mating: A Question of Color

1. Opening quote by Tonya from telephone interview on Jan. 18, 1992.
2. Reference to pattern of color in spouses in Melville Herskovits, *The American Negro* (Bloomington: Indiana University Press, 1968), p. 64.
3. Reference to percentage of Black men and women desiring light-skinned partners in K. B. Clark and M. P. Clark, "What Do Blacks Think of Themselves," *Ebony*, Nov. 1980, pp. 176–82.
4. Reference to eminent men marrying lighter-skinned women in Elisabeth Mullins and Paul Sites, "The Origins of Contemporary Eminent Black Americans: A Three-Generation Analysis of Social Origin," *American Sociological Review* (1984), pp. 672–85.
5. Comment by Marianne Ilaw in telephone interview in March 1992.
6. Spike Lee's comment on light-skinned Black women in Jill Nelson, "'Mo' Better Spike," *Essence*, Aug. 1990, p. 55.
7. Story about Effi Barry in cover story of *Jet*, July 23, 1990.
8. Quote about dark-skinned Black man being called "black bastard" in Calvin Hernton, *Sex and Racism in America* (New York: Grove, 1965), p. 83.
9. Excerpt about Tea Cake and Janie in Zora Neale Hurston, *Their Eyes Were Watching God* (New York: Harper & Row, 1937), pp. 140–41.
10. Analysis of Hurston's book in Alice Walker, "Embracing the Dark and Light in Me," *Essence*, July 1982, pp. 117.
11. Song by Negro punster in C. Eric Lincoln, "Joe Jipson: An Autobiography of a Southern Town," unpublished manuscript. Cited in C. Eric Lincoln, "Color and Group Identity in the United States," 1967, p. 532.
12. Reference about interracial dating during civil rights movement in Paula Giddings, *When and Where I Enter* (New York: William Morrow, 1984), p. 301.
13. Theory that a Black man's desire for a White woman is rooted in rage discussed in William H. Grier and Price M. Cobbs, *Black Rage* (New York: Bantam Books, 1968), p. 91.
14. Comment by sociologist Charles Willie in Isabel Wilkerson, "Black-White Marriages Rise, but Couples Still Face Scorn," *New York Times*, Dec. 2, 1991, B6.
15. Discussion of research by Robert L. Douglas in Michel Marriott, "Colorstruck," *Essence*, Nov. 1991, p. 58.
16. Michel Marriott's comments on his Zimbabwean partner in his "Light-skinned Black Men: Problems and Privileges," *Essence*, Nov. 1988, p. 76.
17. Personal ads in "Personal Dialogue Center" in *The Discovery Center*, Nov. 1991, p. 21.
18. Black-White marriage figures in Sylvester Monroe, "Love in Black and White," *Elle*, Mar. 1992, p. 94.
19. Story of Richard Loving and Mildred Jeter discussed in Wilkerson, "Black-White Marriages Rise."
20. Reference to surveys by National Opinion Research Center in Wilkerson.
21. Quote by Beth Austin in her "Regarding Your Marriage, Your Honor," *Chicago Tribune*, Oct. 6, 1991, Hersay column, sec. 6, p. 11.
22. Statistics on Black women married to White men in Jack Droll with Vern E.

Smith and Andrew Murr, "Spiking a Fever," *Newsweek,* June 10, 1991, pp. 44–46, and Laura B. Randolph, "Black Women/White Men: What's Goin' On?," *Ebony,* Mar. 1989, p. 156.

23. Comment by D. Keith Mano in his "The Black Sex War," *National Review,* Sept. 26, 1986, p. 57.

24. Reference to 20 percent drop in Black marriages in Patrick T. Reardon, "Reasons Sought for Dip in Rate of Black Marriages," *Chicago Tribune,* Nov. 17, 1991, p. 1.

25. Reasons for low number of eligible Black men in cities discussed in *Joliet Times Weekly,* vol. 5, no. 17 (April 24, 1991), p. 2.

26. Quote by White politician's feelings about his interracial relationship in Dorothy Tucker, "Guess Who's Coming to Dinner Now?," *Essence,* April 1987, p. 133.

27. Telephone interview with dark-skinned gay actor named Michael in January 1992.

28. Personal interview with light-skinned gay actor named Eric F. on Dec. 27, 1991.

29. Personal interview with Mary Morten on Nov. 16, 1991.

8: Color Harassment in the Workplace

1. Opening quote from Tracy Morrow's testimony in T. Watson, "Atlanta Woman Asserts Unique Bias in Firing," *Washington Post,* Feb. 22, 1990.

2. Tracy Morrow's story derived and reconstructed from various newspaper articles including "Atlanta Trial Focusing on Color-Bias Charge," *The New York Times,* Feb. 1, 1990, A11; and Michelle Hiskey, "Boss' Skin hue firing unrelated," in *The Atlanta Constitution,* Feb. 1, 1990, C1, as well as from expert witnesses Midge Wilson and Ronald Hall who served on Morrow's behalf.

3. Comments by Dr. Midge Wilson cited in "Pale Skin Spurred Bias, Fired Black Clerk Claims," *Atlanta Journal,* Jan. 31, 1990.

4. Other court cases entailing intraracial color discrimination include EEOC Decision No. 72-04554, EEOC Dec. (CCH) 6496, *Felix* v. *Marquez,* 24 Empl. Prac. Dec. (CCH) 31, at 279 (D.D.C. 1980), *Waller* v. *International Harvester,* 578 F. Supp 309 (D.C. Ill. 1984), *Sere* v. *Board of Trustees of University of Il.,* 628 F. Supp 1548 (N.D. Ill. 1986), dismissed on other grounds, 852 F.2d 285 (7th Cir. 1988), *Saint Francis College et al.* v. *Al-Khazraji,* 481 U.S. 604, 107 S.Ct. 2022, 95, L.Ed.2d 582 (1987), as cited in paper by Kenyatta Tatum, law student, DePaul University, Chicago, 1990.

5. Research by Caroline B. Day published in *A Study of Some Negro-White Families in the United States,* Harvard African Studies, vol. X (Cambridge, 1932), and reported in Otto Klineberg, *Characteristics of the American Negro* (New York: Harper & Row, 1944), p. 346.

6. Quote by Bonnie Allen regarding the hiring of light-skinned Blacks in her "It Ain't Easy Being Pinky," *Essence,* July 1982, p. 68.

7. Discussion of Nimat A. Rashid's color discrimination case in Ann Hardie, "Morehouse Med School Faces EEOC Complaints," *Atlanta Journal Constitution,* Feb. 23, 1990.

8. Personal interview with Benton Harbor public works employees in December 1991.

9. Telephone interview with Mary Walker in May 1992.
10. Reference to hiring of light-skinned females in Allen, "It Ain't Easy Being Pinky," p. 128.
11. Discussion of "pink-collar" jobs in Bernice Lott, *Women's Lives: Themes and Variations in Gender Learning* (Monterey, Calif.: Brooks/Cole Publishing Co., 1987), p. 221.
12. Personal interview with Cheryl Tatum on May 17, 1990.
13. Discussion of beauty demands in the workplace as psychologically damaging to females in Naomi Wolf, *The Beauty Myth: How Images of Beauty Are Used Against Women* (New York: William Morrow, 1991), pp. 20–57.
14. Discussion of pseudofolliculitis can be found in Lawrence K. Altman, "For Some 'No Beards' Is Painful Job Rule," *The New York Times*, Health, Jul. 19, 1990, B8.

9: The Media: Images in Black and Light

1. Opening quote by Queen Shenequa, a fictional character appearing on *Saturday Night Live*, 1991–1992 season.
2. Discussion of "tragic mulatto" genre in telephone interviews with Gary Smith, professor of African-American literature, English Department, DePaul University, Feb. 1992, and William L. Andrews, Joyce and Elizabeth Hall Professor of American Literature, University of Kansas, Feb. 1992.
3. Reference to Harriet Beecher Stowe's *Uncle Tom's Cabin* in *Encyclopedia of Black America*, eds. W. Augustus Low and Virgil A. Clift (New York: Da Capo Paperbacks, McGraw-Hill, 1981), p. 524.
4. Reference to George Washington Cable's *Old Creole Days* in Sterling Brown, "Negro Character as Seen by White Author," *Journal of Negro Education*, vol. 2 (1933), pp. 179–202.
5. Quote by Brown, "Negro Character as Seen by White Author," p. 194.
6. Reference to William Wells Brown's *Clotel* in *Encyclopedia of Black America*, p. 524.
7. Discussion of Harriet Wilson's *Our Nig* in Henry Louis Gates, Jr., Introduction to *Our Nig* (New York: Vintage Books, 1983).
8. Reference to *Iola Leroy* in "The Image of Black Women in Film" in Marianna W. Davis, ed., *Contributions of Black Women to America* (Columbia, S.C.: Kenday Press, 1982), p. 157.
9. Reference to Charles W. Chesnutt's *House Behind the Cedars* in *Encyclopedia of Black America*, p. 525.
10. Reference to Jessie Fauset's educational achievements in *Encyclopedia of Black America*, p. 384.
11. Comment by Truman about mulatto being much nearer White than Black in Wallace Thurman, *The Blacker the Berry* (New York: Macmillan Publishing Co., 1970), p. 146.
12. Reference to Langston Hughes's *Mulatto* in *Encyclopedia of Black America*, p. 533.

13. Poem "Cross" by Langston Hughes in *Selected Poems of Langston Hughes*, New York: Alfred A. Knopf, 1926.

14. Poem "Harlem Sweeties" by Langston Hughes in *Shakespeare in Harlem* (New York: Alfred A. Knopf, 1942), pp. 18–20.

15. Gwendolyn Brooks's poem "The Ballad of Chocolate Mabbie," *Blacks* (Third World Press, 1991), originally published in *A Street in Bronzeville* (New York: Harper & Brothers Publishers, 1945), p. 12.

16. Information on Josephine Baker in Donald Bogle, "Josephine," *Essence*, Feb. 1991, p. 66.

17. Reference to minstrel shows in Daniel J. Leab, "The Gamut from A to B," in his *From Sambo to Superspade: The Black Experience in Motion Pictures* (Boston: Houghton Mifflin, 1975), p. 8.

18. Reference to Eugene Walters's *The Easiest Way* in Leab, *From Sambo to Superspade*, p. 10.

19. Discussion of five roles for Black film actors in Donald Bogle, *Toms, Coons, Mulattoes, Mammies, and Bucks: An Interpretive History of Blacks in American Films* (New York: Viking, 1973).

20. Reference to D. W. Griffith's *Birth of a Nation* in Leab, *From Sambo to Superspade*, pp. 23–39.

21. Reference to D. W. Griffith's *One Exciting Night* in Langston Hughes and Milton Meltzer, *Black Magic: A Pictorial History of the African American in the Performing Arts* (New York: Da Capo Press, 1967), p. 303.

22. Reference to Stepin Fetchit's work to remove racial barriers for Black actors in *Encyclopedia of Black America*, p. 385.

23. Reference to Lincoln Motion Picture Company in Leab, *From Sambo to Superspade*, pp. 64–70.

24. Quote by Jane Gaines in her "The Scar of Shame: Skin Color and Cast in Black Silent Melodrama," *Cinema Journal*, vol. 26 (1987), p. 15.

25. Comment about Oscar Micheaux casting light-skinned Black actors and actresses in Leab, p. 78.

26. Reference to Micheaux' *House Behind the Cedars* and *Homesteader* in Leab, pp. 173–74.

27. Mention of Beavers' salary and Washington's career in Leab, pp. 108–9.

28. Discussion of *Lost Boundaries* in Leab, p. 152.

29. Discussion of *Pinky* in Leab, pp. 153–56.

30. Discussion of 1959 remake of *Imitation of Life* in Leab, p. 212–13.

31. Discussion of Lena Horne's contract and audition in Gail Lumet Buckley, *The Hornes* (New York: Alfred A. Knopf, 1986), pp. 155–57.

32. Discussion of *Island in the Sun* in Leab, pp. 209–11.

33. Comment by angry Black writer calling Poitier a "warmed-over white shirt" in Leab, *From Sambo to Superspade*, p. 230.

34. Discussion of "blaxploitation" films in J. Pines, *Blacks in Film* (London: Studio Vista, 1975), pp. 118–27.

35. Figure on number of blaxploitation films in Davis, *Contributions of Black Women to America*, p. 147.

36. Comments by Debra Pratt on "The Best of Screen Scene," Black Entertainment Television, December 15, 1990.

37. Comment by Rae Dawn Chong on *Arsenio Hall Show*, CBS, Jan. 24, 1991. Reference to Whoopi Goldberg's love scene with Sam Eliot being cut on *Entertainment Tonight*, CBS, May 26, 1992.

38. Comments by filmmaker Zeinabu irene Davis in telephone interview on March 3, 1992.

39. Reference to independent female filmmakers in "Acker, Ally, Arts: Women Behind the Camera," *Ms.*, Mar./Apr. 1992, pp. 64–67.

40. Comments by CORE regarding Vanessa Williams in David Bradley, "Talking with . . . Vanessa Williams," *Redbook*, Feb. 1984, p. 76.

41. Excerpt about Vanessa Williams in Clarence Page, ed., *A Foot in Each World: Essays and Articles by Leanita McClain* (Evanston, Ill.: Northwestern University Press, 1986), p. 44.

42. Quote by Leanita McClain on color prejudice within the Black community in "Beauty Brings Out the Beast" (Sept. 25, 1983), in Page, *A Foot in Each World*, pp. 44–46.

43. Reference to McClain's suicide in Page, p. 3.

44. Reference to Naomi Campbell wearing blond wigs in Deborah Gregory, "They Shoot Models Don't They?," *Essence*, April 1991, p. 47.

45. Telephone interview with Bethann Hardison on Feb. 25, 1992.

46. Number of White and Black models in Gregory, "They Shoot Models Don't They?", p. 47.

47. Data on racism and colorism in advertising in "Race Bias Seen in Magazine Ads," *Invisible People* report, p. 21, and through telephone interview at New York City Department of Consumer Affairs, July 24, 1991.

48. Research on cosmetic ads in Linda Jackson and Kelly Ervin, "The Frequency and Portrayal of Black Females in Fashion Advertisements," *Journal of Black Psychology*, vol. 18, no. 1 (1991), pp. 67–70.

49. Quote by Cynthia Bailey in Susan Howard, "Breaking the Beauty Barrier," *New York Newsday*, May 9, 1990.

50. Telephone interview with Trudy Haynes on Dec. 16, 1991.

51. Comments on rap music in David Samuels, "The Rap on Rap," *New Republic*, Nov. 11, 1991, pp. 24–29.

52. Nelson George's reference to "ghettocentrism" in Samuels, "The Rap on Rap."

53. Telephone interview with Dr. Alvin Poussaint in February 1992.

54. The lyrics of Big Daddy Kane are from the song "Bugged Out Tip" on the LP *Taste of Chocolate*, AZ Music Pub./Cold Chillin' Music, NY, Pub. admin. by Warner/Chappel Music (ASCAP).

55. The song "Dark Skin Girls" can be found on Del Tha flunke Homosapien's album *I Wish My Brother George Was Here*, Electra Entertainment, a division of Warner Communications, 1991.

56. Interpretation of Jermaine Jackson's song "Word to the Badd" in Farai Chideya, "Just Beat It, Brother" in *Newsweek*, November 18, 1991.

57. Teddy Riley's comments on Michael Jackson's plastic surgery in Michael Gold-

berg, "Michael Jackson: The Making of the King of Pop" in *Rolling Stone*, Feb. 1992, p. 37.

58. Quote about Michael Jackson by Michael Goldberg, "Michael Jackson: The Making of the King of Pop" in *Rolling Stone*, Feb. 1992, p. 37.

Epilogue: About Change

1. Opening quotation by Zora Neale Hurston in her "How It Feels to Be Colored Me," in P. C. Hoy II, E. H. Schor, and R. DiYanni, eds., *Women's Voices: Visions and Perspectives* (New York: McGraw-Hill, 1990), p. 649.

2. Quote by George C. Wolfe about *The Colored Museum* in *Essence*, Feb. 1991, People sect., p. 35.

Acknowledgments

Collectively, we wish to thank our literary agent, Julian Bach, and our editor, Alane Mason, for having faith in this project even when we did not. We would also like to express our appreciation to Celia Wren for her editorial assistance.

Individually, Kathy Russell thanks her mom Dorothy for her love and inspiration, and Dr. Michael I. Senegal for his unfailing enthusiasm and support, Bertice Berry for her friendship and invaluable insight, Peter McDonald for his many votes of confidence and much-needed comic relief, Shaun Reynolds for his infinite knowledge and wisdom and his world-class pancakes, and the friends and family who assisted her in helping to make this book happen.

Midge Wilson thanks the chairman of her psychology department, Sheldon Cotler, and DePaul University for its institutional support. She also thanks her research assistants, Sherry Salmons and Kathie Castle, the helpful office staff, most especially Nancy Rospenda and Lucinda Rapp, colleagues Rod Watts, Gary Smith, Sandra Jackson, Lillie Edwards, Richard DeCordeva, and Lisa Razzano for their patience and insight, rap consultant Jaleel Abdul-Adil, Angela Neal, who first introduced her to the subject of colorism, and all her buddies, especially the Sunday night bowlers, who kept her spirits up when her energy flagged. Finally, she thanks her parents, Marge and Jimmie Wilson, for being there at the conception.

Ronald Hall thanks Richard Majors, Richard Lyle, Richard Allen, Mamie Darlington, LaVern Ford, Harriet Steele, Lloyd S. Jolley, Patricia Johnson, Janice Vaughn, and Gilmary Best.

Permissions
and Copyrights

Written permission was obtained from all interviewees who provided material for this book. Where noted, names of interviewees have been changed, as well as other persons they named who could be harmed by their disclosures.

1. Two verses from the poem "The Ballad of Chocolate Mabbie" by Gwendolyn Brooks in *Blacks,* Third World Press, 1991. © Gwendolyn Brooks, 1991.
2. Excerpt from Sara Lawrence Lightfoot, *Balm in Gilead* © 1988 by Sara Lawrence Lightfoot. Reprinted with permission of Addison-Wesley Publishing Company.
3. Excerpt from *Black Rage* © 1968 by William Grier and Price Cobbs. Reprinted with permission of Basic Books, division of Harper Collins, Inc.
4. Excerpt from Wallace Thurman, *The Blacker The Berry* (New York: Macmillan, 1970)
5. Excerpt from *The Bluest Eye* © 1970 by Toni Morrison and reprinted with permission of Toni Morrison.
6. Excerpt from "Bugged Out Tip" by Big Daddy Kane from *Taste of Chocolate* LP © 1991. Reprinted with permission of AZ Music Pub./Cold Chillin' Music, Pub. administered by Warner/Chappel Music (ASCAP).
7. Excerpt from *Certain People* by Stephen Birmingham © 1977 and reprinted with permission of Little, Brown, and Company.
8. Excerpt from *Chicago Tribune* article "Regarding Your marriage, Your Honor" by Beth Austin reprinted with permission of author.
9. Excerpt from *The Hungry Mind Review* article "Life with Daughters or The Cakewalk with Shirley Temple," by Gerald Early reprinted with permission of author, and *The Hungry Mind Review,* copyright © 1991, St. Paul, MN,
10. Excerpt from *Cinema Journal* article "The Scar of Shame: Skin Color and Cast in Black Silent Melodrama" by Jane Gaines © 1987 by the Board of Trustees of the University of Illinois. Reprinted by permission of the University of Illinois Press.
11. Excerpt from *Color and Race* edited by John H. Franklin in chapter "Color, Racism, and Christianity" by Roger Bastide © 1968 reprinted by permission of *Daedalus:* the Journal of the American Academy of Arts and Sciences.
12. Excerpt from the poem "Cross" from *Selected Poems* by Langston Hughes, Copyright 1926 by Alfred A. Knopf, Inc. and renewed 1954 by Langston Hughes. Reprinted by permission of the publisher.
13. Excerpt of lyrics of "Dark Skin Girls" by Sidney Barnes, Theresa Lindsey, George Clinton, and Teren Delvon Jones copyright © 1991, reprinted with permission from Stone Agate Music/Street Knowledge Music.
14. Excerpt from *Drylongso: A Self-Portrait of Black America* by John Langston

Index

626/590-0786